BEYOND BASIC DOG TRAINING

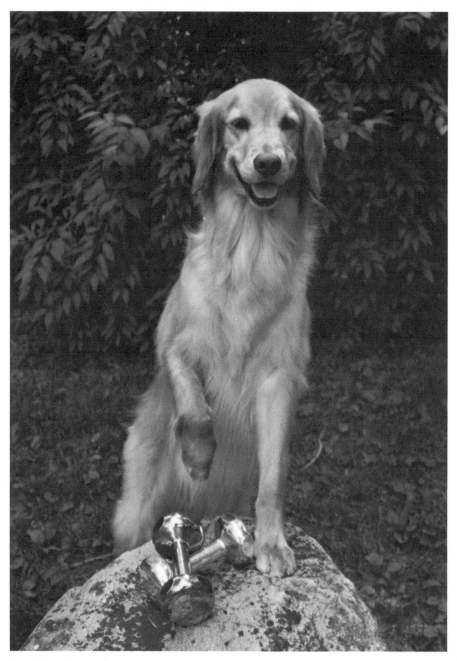

O.T. Ch. Meadowpond Fem De Fortune, W.C. "Charo" is a three-time Gaines Superdog winner. She is a member of the Golden Retriever Obedience Hall of Fame and retired with six perfect scores of 200. Charo is owned, trained, and loved by Diane Bauman.

Beyond Basic Dog Training

by Diane L. Bauman

First Edition—Fifth Printing
1988

HOWELL BOOK HOUSE Inc.
230 Park Avenue
New York, N.Y. 10169

Library of Congress Cataloging-in-Publication Data

Bauman, Diane L.
  Beyond basic dog training.

  1. Dogs—Training. I. Title.
SF431.B37 1986   636.7'08'8   86-7234
ISBN 0-87605-409-2

FOR MY FATHER
whose last words to me
before he died were
"Write the book—
it's important."

Author Diane Bauman together with a group of outstanding obedience performers trained by her methods.

Fred Stevenson

Table of Contents

Foreword

YOU ARE ABOUT to embark on an adventure in dog obedience as only Diane Bauman can take you. Her remarkable ability to view training from the dog's perspective has enabled her to create a style so pervasive that it will enchant even the most seasoned of trainers.

Clear understanding has led Diane to the development of training methods which afford dog and handler a relationship of powerful communication.

It is a refreshing realization that our canine companions have a higher level of intelligence than is traditionally granted.

Many dogs labeled unmanageable, dangerous or just unwanted have been rescued by Diane. Once adopted and trained by her they developed a new outlook on life and were later carefully placed in new homes to become happy companions or obedience competitors.

The author's brilliance as a trainer, together with her extraordinary talent as a teacher make it a privilege to be her student.

I'm sure I speak for many when I thank Diane for so generously revealing her secrets and ideas that have developed over many years of experience and intuitive thought.

Clearly much time, devotion and effort have gone into making this book a pleasure to read. *Beyond Basic Dog Training* will be an invaluable source of reference to read and re-read with each and every chapter essential. My favorite part of this book is the conclusion, where my heart skipped a few beats. I believe that this is where Diane has captured the true meaning of "dog training."

—Laurie Rubenfeld

Laurie Rubenfeld is an active participant in the sport of dog obedience and has been training with the author for approximately three years as *Beyond Basic Dog Training* goes to press.

Acknowledgments

THE PAGES that follow hold my thoughts about training dogs. These thoughts combine ideas developed from books, seminars, other trainers, dogs themselves and original thought. I have been very fortunate to have known some very knowledgeable and generous people. For their continued support and appreciation of my endeavors, I thank some who have made this book possible: Nancy Overton, Bill and Mary Chaillot, Margaret Fitch, Dr. H. L. Yandell, Larry Schillenkamp, Jack Godsil, Bob Self, Marly Whiting, Alfred Einhorn, Sheila Eckstein, Ruth Rosbach, Jeff Bauman, my parents, students and every dog's leash that has ever passed through my hands.

Of all those who helped shape my training methods, Ruth Rosbach (my partner) has had the greatest influence. Her intuitive understanding of people and dogs and her undying humor helped this book take shape. Thank you, Ruth, for all you have given me in so many ways.

Introduction

THIS BOOK was written with the best interests of dogs in mind. The author believes it is time to go beyond *training* dogs and start *teaching* them how to please us. Assuming that dogs are capable of reasoning and simple problem solving, the author feels dogs need not be trained as if they were merely simple stimulus-response mice.

The teaching methods presented encourage and cultivate dogs' cognitive abilities. Believing that dogs learn by trial and error, the author encourages dogs by removing corrections for incorrect responses. As a result, the dogs do not fear failure and are taught to exercise options in a quest for the desired behavior. The concept that "wrong is wonderful" when teaching dogs is new to the world of competitive dog trainers.

Diane Bauman's novel "teaching" approach has produced many top obedience performers in many breeds. They exhibit confident, alert, accurate, enthusiastic style in the obedience ring. In her own words, "Their minds have been stimulated while their egos have been left intact. They are happy to be doing what they understand."

Diane Bauman is an internationally known obedience instructor and has given obedience clinics all over the United States and Canada. Her articles have appeared in *Off-Lead* magazine and *Front and Finish: The Dog Trainers' News.* Her obedience demonstrations have been televised in New York and California. Diane is owner/trainer of the famous Golden Retriever O.T. Ch. Meadowpond Fem de Fortune, W.C., winner of the Gaines Superdog title three times while achieving the highest Superdog average ever. The author's record boasts eight perfect 200 scores earned on three different dog breeds.

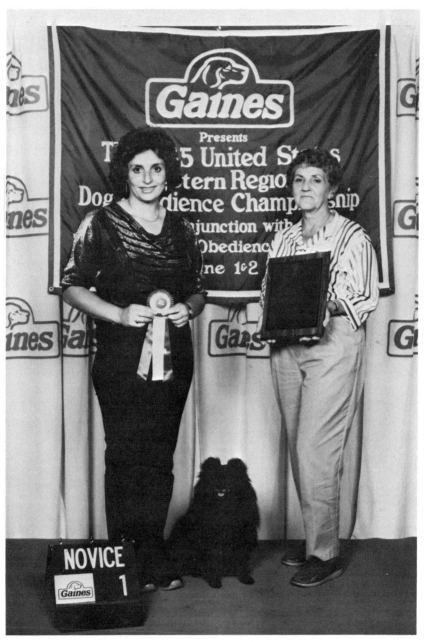

Diane Bauman and Pomeranian Noah's Abra Ka Dabra, C.D. shown winning the Novice Division of the 1985 Gaines Eastern Regional. Abra was rescued from Noah's Ark Animal Shelter at the age of three years. At the age of four she was awarded the top Novice Dog in the Eastern Region.

Godsil

1

Training the Thinking Dog

DOG TRAINING, like religion, embraces different beliefs based on different premises resulting in different training methods. When you consider that obedience fans go to trials on Sundays and often resort to prayer, the analogy is further strengthened! Many trainers tell students to verbally scold and others advocate "no verbal harshness." Some say to yell "no" and others believe this is unnecessary. There are those who tell you to starve your dog, feed your dog, snap your dog, love your dog, and some who will even suggest you get a new dog! If you read enough books and attend enough seminars, you'll go crazy searching for the "right" way to train dogs! A training method is only successful for you if you fully understand it and feel comfortable with it.

One thing I have learned over the years of training my own dogs and instructing others is that dogs will learn in spite of what is done to them! This is both encouraging and misleading. Encouraging because it means that if you hack away long enough your dog will eventually learn it (providing he lives long enough) but misleading because many ridiculous methods of training dogs have developed and the dogs eventually responded even though the methods made no sense. If you scratch your head just before your dog does a fast sit, does this mean that scratching your head should become a method used to teach fast sits?

To complicate matters further, good dog trainers are always changing their methods! They remain open to new ideas and search for more effective techniques. Trainers who resist change and lose creativity in their training become stagnant and limited. They often resent and resist new ideas; it is easier to resist than to change.

The only thing trainers agree on is that there is no one way to teach something. I have heard it said that if the method works, it's a good method. There was a time I agreed with this philosophy, but after watching dogs trained different ways, I now feel that how you teach something can be as important as the fact that the dog learns it. The end does not always justify the means.

A child is told by a parent that he must get good grades or severe consequences will follow. If the child is not naturally intelligent, he might work himself into exhaustion or a nervous breakdown or might even resort to cheating to get the grades. At the end of the year, he has received the grades but has lost his integrity, mental stability and health in doing so.

The dog who slowly slinks out to retrieve a dumbbell is a dog who has not been trained with the best possible methods. The dog who heels with his head down, lagging three feet (or more, sometimes) behind his owner, was not born this way; this poor heeling was caused by poor training. While the dog may be "heeling," the method used was perhaps not the best approach.

There are people who look at the depressed, lagging, slinky dog and immediately analyze, "Aha, this dog has been beaten—isn't it awful that people could do such a thing!" I have seen many dogs heel in a pitiful manner and know of very few books or training schools that advocate beating a dog to teach him to heel. I also know of very few concerned dog owners who would beat their dogs even if told to do so. So why the pitiful lagging? While the dog has not been abused physically, poor training has abused him mentally. The trainer did not clearly *explain* to the dog what was expected, but he did correct him for what he had not yet learned. The method lacked clarity, fairness and motivation.

While heeling will be covered in detail later, let me whet your appetite. If you are trying to teach a dog what heel position is, why would you give him enough leash to get out of heel position? Now you have to correct him for what he has not yet learned. How can we correct a dog for being wrong before we teach him what right is? And finally, how can you expect a dog to heel perfectly if you, the handler, can't walk a straight line and stick your feet out to trip the dog on about turns?

In the pages that follow I have outlined training methods that make sense to me and to my dogs. It is not the purpose of this book to teach you to train your dog for I truly believe that you cannot train a dog to its full potential from a book. The objective is to get you, the owner, handler, trainer of your little "furry friend" to THINK about what you are doing and why you are doing it, for it is only a thinking handler who can train the thinking dog!

2

Wrong Is Wonderful

A "THINKING DOG" is a confident, happy working animal who understands fully what he is expected to do on any given command, enjoys meeting new challenges, is rarely bored with obedience and can be fine-tuned to the utmost accuracy. He has been guided and trained in such a way that he is not afraid to be wrong. Yes, folks, contrary to much of what you have been told or read, I want my dogs to be wrong. There are trainers who believe the dog is nothing more than a stimulus-response animal which does not have the ability to reason; others maintain that the dog has reasoning capabilities beyond that of a simple animal.

The training that evolves from the first premise is what I refer to as *pattern training*. Sequences of commands are repeated over and over again until the dog performs them on one command. A pattern trainer would teach a broad jump, for example, by setting up a situation where the dog couldn't be wrong and by having the dog repeat the jump many times. Does pattern training get results? You bet it does! It produces non-thinking, fast responding, good-working dogs. The drawback, however, of a pattern-trained dog is that if the pattern is broken by a distraction or by a new situation, the dog is at a loss to perform the task. For example, the pattern-trained dog is taught to retrieve a dumbbell quickly—get out there, grab it and get back. He has done this so many times that he hardly has to think about what he's doing. He would probably even retrieve on any command if it followed the sequence of stay, throw dumbbell, send. One day the dumbbell goes under the ring gate. The pattern-trained dog runs out for his dumbbell and is faced with a problem. Since he cannot complete the patterned response and has not been taught while practicing the exercise to reason, he runs out, indicates the dumbbell, but comes back without it. Another example of pattern training is the dog which is taught the high jump by jumping it over and over again as his owner runs alongside with him. Then, when owner and dog are in an obedience trial performing off-lead heeling and the judge calls a fast along side the high jump, the dog goes over the jump. Even though no command was given, the dog remembered the high jump pattern. Pattern-trained dogs have more problems with the Drop-On-Recall exercise and in distinguishing between a Retrieve-Over-the-High-Jump and a Retrieve-on-Flat than do dogs trained to think.

The Drop-On-Recall exercise is perhaps the most difficult exercise to pattern train because the pattern changes. Sometimes the pattern is to drop and sometimes the pattern omits the drop. For a pattern-trained dog, this exercise can be a nightmare for both dog and handler. Dogs trained not to think will often be seen doing very fast, impressive drops but also frequently anticipating drops. Every dog which has ever learned a drop on recall is going to anticipate at some point in training. How you work through the anticipation (either to pattern past it, often with repeated recalls on a longline, or to teach the dog to understand the exercise by reasoning it out) determines whether the dog will *continue* to anticipate a drop. Pattern trainers talk about "only dropping the dog in the ring" to avoid anticipation. Trainers of thinking dogs frequently drop their dogs in practice with no ill effects because the dogs understand the exercise and are confidently waiting for the signal or command to drop.

An alternative to pattern training is practiced by trainers who believe dogs are capable of reasoning and who want dogs to think before reacting. Most guide-dog trainers also approach training in this manner. A guide dog is forever being faced with new situations—he must be able to reason and to solve simple problems. Trainers who teach dogs to think believe that dogs learn by trial and error and that when a dog is wrong, that is wonderful because when he exhausts all the wrong possibilities he will then be right. Wrong is never "bad," it is just wrong. Future guide dogs are repeatedly allowed to make their own mistakes. In fact, the trainers set up situations which will cause mistakes, without the intention of correcting the dog! In guide work, a slow-moving car is planted and the dog is allowed to walk a person into the car. The trainer bangs on the car to make noise, but *no correction* is given to the dog. This is how the dog learns what happens and later avoids moving vehicles. The dog is not reprimanded for being wrong. If you reprimand a dog when it is wrong, it then becomes afraid to be wrong ("fear of failure"). A dog which is afraid to make a mistake becomes so panicked that learning is impaired. For example, when learning Directed Jumping, if the dog takes the wrong jump and is yelled at, it will often resort to not jumping at all. If, on the other hand, the dog is permitted to come over the wrong jump but receives no praise as the owner continues to stand there with his arm pointing to the right jump, the dog will realize that something is wrong yet not be afraid to try again. I have seen many dogs go back out without another command and fix their own mistake, but these were dogs which had been taught from the beginning that it is okay to be wrong and to try another approach.

A thinking dog is taught to listen. A dumbbell is thrown, and the handler commands "HEEL" instead of "TAKE IT." A thinking dog does what it is told and does not do what the sight picture might indicate. Thinking dogs derive a lot of pleasure from solving problems on their own. They are more confident, consistent workers and rarely get bored with obedience.

If you'd like to know what type of training you've been doing, try this experiment. Tell your dog to stay, walk out 15 feet and show the dog that you are placing a dumbbell on the ground. Then walk another 15 feet and turn to face your dog as though it were a Recall exercise. Command your dog to "TAKE IT." (No pointing permitted.) Do not be surprised if he comes straight to you on a recall because he was not thinking and was responding to a patterned situation. If he makes this mistake, DON'T CORRECT HIM! Help explain it to him by saying nothing and by walking slowly back while pointing to the dumbbell. When he finally picks up the dumbbell, praise profusely and try again. You may shorten the distances if he repeatedly does it wrong.

People who teach dogs to think never get upset when the dog is repeatedly wrong. They know that when the "light goes on" and the dog understands, he will no longer make the mistake. Pattern trainers, on the other hand, get very upset when a dog is wrong because they fear patterning an undesired response. Pattern trainers rush to correct mistakes, often frightening the dog, in an effort to avoid a bad pattern of behavior. Trainers of thinking dogs, on the other hand, take their time when correcting because they want the dog to see what happens when he is "good, but wrong." Thinking dogs are never seen running from their owners after a mistake because they are *not afraid to be wrong.*

Every time a dog breaks a Sit Stay and is gently put back into position, he has learned something. If he coincidentally remains sitting, or does so because you prevent a mistake, he never really understands the exercise. Most good trainers want dogs to be wrong on Sit Stays during early training, but this approach is abandoned in advanced work.

Not all dogs can be taught to reason as easily as others. For some breeds, perhaps, pattern training is the better approach. While a pattern-trained dog is capable of a superb performance on any given day, thinking dogs are much more consistent, reliable workers. It takes longer to train a thinking dog. Is it worth it?

3

Good News and Bad News

I HAVE GOOD NEWS for you and I have bad news. The good news is that this book has a lot to offer a person currently training dogs. The bad news is that it will not teach you to train your dog. This is not to say that you should give up reading books on training, but understand that it is impossible for the author of a book to offer every possible response to a dog's action, primarily because he can't see the dog react. A book can tell you what to do, what to say, what hand to use and what order to do this in. A book cannot assure that you will say things in the right tone, with the right volume, do things with the right timing and, most importantly, refrain from doing something because the dog is reacting poorly to it. A book will not teach you to read a dog, that is to say judge from the dog's body English what he is thinking.

Trainers have tried to explain obedience in very simple terms. If the dog is right, he is praised and/or rewarded. If he is wrong, he is corrected. It would be easy if training really were this simple, but it is not.

What about the dog who is confused or afraid? Is he to be corrected the same as the dog who knows what you want and was distracted or feels he has a choice? What if the methods offered by the book don't cause the result the book predicted? A book can never tell you what to do for every response.

The purpose of this book is to encourage you to evaluate your current training methods and to consider alternate approaches after understanding the reasons why these approaches have been chosen.

The methods described in this book have been evaluated based on the fact that they work on many different breeds when employed by inexperienced as well as experienced trainers. My own dogs and students' dogs indicate that these techniques produce an extremely reliable, accurate, secure, enthusiastic working dog. Our dogs exhibit animation because they are comfortable with their understanding of what is expected of them. This animation should not be confused with dogs who work with incredible speed that is a result of panic. A dog who never knows when or if he is going to be corrected can appear to be very flashy when in fact he is really

18

nervous. While nervous dogs are often impressive in the ring, their performance is far less consistent compared to that of a calm, thinking animal.

The training methods explained in this book will change slightly as I continue to train. The day a person stops learning from his dogs and his students is the day he loses interest in the sport of obedience. The "how to" section of this book is included with the hope that you will compare these methods to the ones you currently use, notice the differences and question why you are doing things the way you are. It is not the intention of this book to convert anyone to these training methods, only to stimulate *thoughtful* training.

4

Honesty—The Best Policy

ONE OF THE BASIC PREMISES of this training method requires that you always be honest with your dog. When he is right, let him know he is right. When he is wrong, let him know that he is wrong (and that it is okay to be wrong). I have seen handlers who will praise a dog for sitting crooked because it was better than the sit before. Dogs cannot comprehend "better." A dog only understands right or wrong, yes or no. When you praise a dog for being better but not right, you confuse him.

I'm sure you've seen the person who calls his dog to come on a Recall and the dog stands up and doesn't move. The owner yells, "Good boy, hurry!" Well, he is not good for only standing when you said "COME," and how do you hurry a stand, anyway?

Perhaps the greatest damage is done while heeling. A dog lags and his owner, in an attempt to encourage, says, "That's it, cummon, good boy, let's go." Since it all sounds like praise to the dog, the dog assumes he is correct and lags worse. This frustrates the owner who gets angry, which the dog doesn't understand. Finally, the owner yells obscenities at the dog, and the poor dog feels so rejected he no longer wants to even try. The end result is the "hang-dog" look we often see in a ring.

What about the handler who calls his dog to come on a Recall, and the dog comes in briskly and sits front. The handler then says, "Good boy! Get it straight!" While the handler might have intended the praise to be for the Recall, it came after the Sit. To the dog, if the Sit was praised, why is he being told to "Get it straight?" You cannot praise a Sit which you then decide to fix!

Reserve the words "GOOD" or "TERRIFIC" for the correct action. The dog has learned from early training that certain words (different for each dog) mean he has succeeded. Be careful to save these words for only the correct behavior. If you feel the need to encourage an attempt by the dog, try cheering, "Yeeeah!" or words like "Attaboy, you can do it!" Praise a perfectly completed exercise or part of an exercise; encourage an attempt. When a dog lags, tell him in no uncertain terms to "Get up here! Let's go!" Your tone should be calmly demanding and in no way confused with approval. I'm sure you do not approve of lagging so be honest with him.

Lying to your dog never pays! You cannot praise a dog into doing what you want, you must teach him. You cannot "happy him up"; he will be happy when he is secure with his understanding of what is expected of him. Bribing him with tidbits is only a temporary remedy. Eventually he must perform because you tell him to and he understands what is expected of him. Food training is becoming more and more popular among competitive trainers. I guess you could say it's the current trend. There is certainly a time and a place for food rewards in training, but be careful not to rely on food as an answer to all problems. As soon as treats come on the obedience scene, the dog's thoughts are on the food and are no longer focused on the exercise. Perhaps my biggest difficulty with using food in training is because when used as a bribe it is not honest. The dog responds to the drop signal and in practice receives a tidbit. He then does the same thing in the ring and is not rewarded. Unfair! I am never going to be able to reward my dog with food in a ring. Since praise is permitted in the ring, I prefer to train with praise. A combination of food rewards *and praise,* used in moderation, can be very effective in early training, but you will be better off if you wean the dog off the food. (Note: For specific problems where the dog is overly anxious, food rewards do seem to help the dog over his anxiety attack but should be discontinued when the anxiety dissipates.)

In keeping with the concept of being honest with your dog, it would not be fair to correct a dog before he made a mistake. While there are trainers who advocate automatic corrections, I feel this works to destroy an honest working relationship with your dog. For a dog to work confidently, he should feel that he will not be unfairly or automatically corrected. There is no doubt that automatic corrections solve training problems, but at what cost? Why upset your partner if it's not necessary? There are other fair ways to solve the same problems.

5

Slow Down and Shut Up!

THE APPROACH TO TRAINING DOGS in this book is accurately described in a phrase initiated by one of my students, "Slow down and shut up!" When people learn to touch-type, an activity which becomes automatic, they start off by thinking hard and pushing the keys slowly. With time and repetition, they get faster and faster. In fact, if you observe people closely any time they are deeply involved in thought, their motor activity slows down. This information is critical when we talk in terms of training a thinking dog. If you want your dog to think and understand what he is doing, you cannot pressure him with speed in the beginning of the learning process. Teach the dog slowly and let him perform at whatever speed he is comfortable with. After he is reacting confidently to a command, and exhibits understanding, it is safe to push for speed.

A perfect example of a dog slowing down to think is found when teaching the Drop-On-Recall exercise. As soon as you begin dropping a dog on a Recall, the Recall is going to slow down because the dog is thinking about when to drop. The more you have pressured him to drop with speed (prompted by a "flashed signal"), the more fear he has of being wrong, the slower he will come in on a Recall. If you get no Recall at all, consider that you may have pressured the dog beyond the point of good training. The trainer who can't bear to see a dog coming in slowly and tries to speed him up with verbal encouragement or lead corrections (long line) is gambling with both upsetting the dog and preventing the dog from thinking through the exercise. What is so awful about a dog who is coming in slowly (or crouched) because he is thinking about dropping and doesn't want to miss the command or signal? All of my dogs have at one time in practice come in very slowly on the Recall because they were concerned with the drop, but after they learn when to drop and when not to, and when they are not afraid of missing a signal (because the signal is clearly given and not flashed), they all pick up their speed on recall to what it was before the drop was introduced. There are exercises you can incorporate into the teaching of the Drop-On-Recall which help to get the dog up off the drop quickly and things you can do to speed up your basic recalls. These techniques will be discussed in detail in the "how to" section of this book. (See Chapter 34 - *Teaching the Drop-On-Recall* and Chapter 17 - *Special Small Dog and Big Dog Techniques*.)

Your voice can be a valuable training tool, but too much talking can cause problems. I advocate teaching every exercise by giving a command *one time* and then enforcing it. A familiar phrase to our beginning students is, "SIT, SIT is a NO, NO." Sometimes I will turn to someone who has just repeated "SIT" three times and question, "How many dogs did you say you were training?" As soon as you repeat a command, you have effectively told the dog that the first command didn't count. In addition to the fact that AKC trials only permit one command, to repeat yourself confuses a dog. The dog really doesn't know which "SIT" is the *real* "SIT!" Trainers who advocate repeating commands talk about letting the command "sink in." I'm still trying to decide what they think the dog's brain is made of, sand?

Repeating something has never made it easier to understand. Saying it louder has never helped to clarify its meaning, and certainly correcting confusion only makes it worse. If I were to start commanding you to "scubernog," and when you didn't respond I snapped your wrist with a choke chain, and each time you didn't respond I commanded "scubernog" louder and snapped harder, how would you feel? Would you now understand the meaning of "scubernog?" When you arbitrarily command a dog to heel and then snap him for being out of position, are you not doing the same thing? When you repeat the command "HEEL!" loudly and forcefully while the dog is moving (and thinking he is heeling), does this help define the meaning of Heel? If you repeat "HEEL" two thousand times, does this teach him how to heel? NO! For more effective techniques, see Chapter 22 - *Teaching the Dog to Heel.*

The philosophy of giving only one command is very effective when teaching the Sit-Stay. Tell the dog to "SIT," he does, and then you command "STAY" and leave him. If the dog breaks the Stay and gets up, reposition and praise him, but no extra "SIT" or "STAY" commands are necessary. My feeling is that if I keep reminding the dog to Sit and Stay why should he bother to remember it? By the time the dog is in Open he must remember what he's doing for three and five minutes. All too often dogs break Stays because they forget what they are doing. By placing the dog into the Sit and praising him for being there and then leaving without a second command, the burden of thought is now placed on the dog. He must *THINK* about what he is doing and work to remember it if he is to avoid correction. No one is going to be there to keep telling him to Sit and Stay. Some of you may be doubting your dog's ability to learn without the repetition of commands. Give dogs more credit for intelligence and you may be surprised to find they won't let you down. Of course, if you never challenge their thinking abilities, you'll never know their potential.

Perhaps the most important time to remain quiet is when the dog is moving away from you, as in the Retrieve or Go-Out exercises. I have seen dogs leave their owners' sides at a nice speed, only to hear the owner command, "Hurry!" and the dog stops and turns back as if to say, "What did you say?" The clearest example of this was a student of mine who was teaching Go-Outs to her dog who had a tendency to stop short. One day she sent the dog out and just before the dog reached the point where she usually stopped, the owner shrieked, "Ginger, don't stop there!" Ginger turned on her name and sat facing her owner with her tail wagging a mile a minute. She was so pleased that she had finally taught her owner where to stop her!

Another time to be quiet is whenever the dog is thinking. I am sure that at some time you were trying to concentrate while some well-meaning person insisted on talking to you. Dogs find chatter distracting. In a case where a dog has to work to get a dumbbell out from under a gate, be quiet and let him do it by himself. When he succeeds, then you can become hysterical with joy and praise. If a dog starts for a jump in the Directed Jumping exercise and then stops because he's not sure (early training stages), use your arm, your body, your facial expression, any kind of pantomime but, if at all possible, avoid double commanding. Letting a dog work out his problems is much more advantageous than doing all the work for him or repeating commands. Dogs get a great deal of satisfaction when they have figured something out. When the trainer is simply repeating a command over and over again, dogs tend to get bored or frightened and tune out or give up.

6

A "Pity Party" for Rover
or Little People in Fur Coats

DOGS LEARN to be manipulative at an early age. They quickly realize that a pitiful, hangdog look or sad whimpering results in a tidbit of food from the table. If this behavior is allowed to continue, your dog will have you convinced that he is unable to do anything you ask. The "pitiful dog" act, which is learned by the dog through trial and error, is often seen in obedience.

Handlers who love their dogs are easily made to feel guilty about commanding the dog to perform. Usually when you find a depressed looking dog, there is a guilty handler nearby!

You really have no reason to ever feel guilty about asking your dog to obey. You love him, feed him, house him, provide for his health, education, and take him on vacations. As Jack Godsil used to say, "You find me a job where I get room, board, education, entertainment, medical care, grooming, vacations, and I only have to work 20 minutes a day and occasional weekends, and I'll take it!" Our dogs live a wonderful life. I do not believe that three minutes of attentive heeling in a ring is too much to ask.

Most dogs will put forth as little effort as is necessary to perform a task. Good jumpers will clear a 24-inch jump by one inch as well as clear a 36-inch jump by one inch. If you want your dog to reach his full potential in obedience, you will have to learn to "sweetly demand." You can be a very demanding trainer without ever raising your voice by being consistent, fair, honest and liberal with praise. If, on the other hand, you are waiting for the dog to give of himself, simply to please you, you are waiting for a very special dog you may never meet.

At the risk of shattering dreams, I must state that I do not believe dogs obey because they wish to please man or because they love you. They may love you, but this has no bearing on how they perform obedience. A dog obeys because it is *to his advantage* to do so, either because you will lavish him with praise, and thus feed his ego, or because by obeying he avoids a correction.

How do I know this to be true? If you are housebreaking a puppy and every time he has an accident you turn to him and say, "Sweetheart, you're breaking my heart. I love you. How could you do this to me?" would the dog become housebroken? If, on the other hand, every time you catch the dog having an accident you lift him up and put him outside, will he not learn? If someone picked you up in the middle of going to the bathroom, would you not think twice about going in that spot again?

If you are to become an effective trainer, it is important that you make an effort to view life through the eyes of a dog.

Attributing human characteristics to our canines, while cute, hinders our ability to train. While I may live with "little people in fur coats," when I train, I train dogs.

Shed your guilt and learn to *demand*, sweetly.

7

Demand Sweetly

HAVE YOU EVER NOTICED that you can follow instructions exactly, perform every step with perfect timing and coordination and still you can't get your dog to respond the way your instructor can? In addition to learning *what* to do and *when* to do it, there is something I call "attitude" which is a key ingredient if anything you learn is to be effective. Attitude is something which develops in time and with experience.

By the time you train your second dog you have no doubt that you can teach a dog to Sit and Stay. You approach the teaching of these exercises with a calm confidence which the dog senses. If the dog resists, you do not become flustered because there is no doubt in your mind that you can teach the dog to Sit. You are patient, insistent and sweetly demanding because your confidence allows you to be.

On the other hand, the first time you attempted to teach a dog to Sit, you were not so sure you could do it. If the dog resisted, you became flustered, insecure, often embarrassed. The dog, sensing your insecurity and uneasiness, became more resistant.

In both cases you applied the exact same methods, with perfect timing, coordination and voice control, and you got two different responses because of *your* attitude. You can't force yourself to become confident, but you can gain confidence by training with someone whom you trust totally to lead you through the woods to the U.D. (Utility Degree) at the end of the path.

I always assure my students that it only gets easier and each subsequent dog they train gets better. Knowing in your heart that you *can* do it makes all the difference in the world. Whenever possible, appear secure, confident and in control to your dog. You are always better off doing the wrong thing affirmatively than doing the right thing tentatively.

If your instructor makes *you* feel insecure, find a new instructor because "the blind leading the blind" doesn't get you very far.

8

Where to Go to Train

IT HAS BEEN SAID that a school is only as good as the teacher your child has. Whether you choose to take private or group classes or train with a school or a club, the most important element is the knowledge, experience and ability to teach of the person you are learning from. Unfortunately, there is no formal education or licensing required for someone to advertise as a DOG TRAINER. As a result, many people teaching obedience today are barely qualified.

If you are interested in showing your dog in obedience trials, learn from someone who is actively competing and doing well. Choose someone whose style of handling his dog you admire. If you are by nature a soft-spoken person, you will never feel comfortable taking lessons from someone who issues commands like a marine drill instructor. No, you do not have to sound authoritative or angry to get response from a dog. Any command is only as effective as it is enforced. Threatening commands have never worked any better than sweet, enforced commands. Try to find an instructor who has had some experience with your breed or similar size of breed. Make sure your instructor has trained at least through a U.D. (Utility Dog) degree, even though you are starting with Beginners, for a good foundation is essential to advanced training. Beginners is really Beginning Utility and should be taught as such. If your instructor has never trained a UD dog, he may not be aware of the things you learn in Beginners that will affect future training. For example, if you are taught to give a Stay command with your right hand in Beginners, when you get to Utility are you going to give a Stand also with your right hand? And, if you use your left hand for the Stand, what hand will give the Heel command? To give clear, logical signals, Stay should always be given with your left hand from Beginners through Utility, but if an instructor has never been in Utility, he would not be aware of this.

There should be a reason for everything you do with your dog, and your instructor should welcome your questions and be able to answer why you are using a particular method. By the way, just because it works is not a good enough reason. Good instructors have numerous methods to teach the same exercise. An instructor who repeatedly tells you to "go home and work on it" or "you need to do it for another two weeks before you will get any results" is perhaps not versatile enough for your dog.

Before you can train a dog for competition, you must have a mental picture of what you are working towards. My first Open dog did the Drop-On-Recall exercise the way he had been taught. He came at a trot, lay down, waited for another command to come and trotted briskly to me. For a year I was quite pleased with his Drop-On-Recall. One day I went to an obedience seminar and saw a dog perform a Drop-On-Recall with such speed and style that I was amazed. The dog dropped so fast and remained so attentive to his owner that it didn't even resemble the same exercise I was teaching. From then on my mental picture of the Drop-On-Recall exercise was different, and not only was I able to improve the performance of my first dog, but every dog following has been trained to the new mental picture. It is an advantage to be able to take lessons from someone who can help provide you with good mental pictures or, at the very least, has the picture of the perfect exercise clearly in mind. For the sake of the mental picture, it is advantageous to attend the Gaines Regionals and Classics to watch the most highly trained dogs and handlers in the country perform every year.

If you live in an area where there is no one teaching classes who meets the description I have outlined, you can do it on your own. Dog training is logical—it should make sense. Trust your instincts and evaluate your results. The old cliche "necessity is the mother of invention" has produced some excellent training methods. Thinking handlers who work alone often achieve more than non-questioning students who are spoon-fed by the unqualified. One of the most thinking handlers I have ever met came from a small mining town in the mountains of Colorado and only had one other person to train with. She didn't know all the answers, but she was asking all the right questions.

Have you ever noticed that someone who is really proficient at a skill makes it appear simple? The same is true of dog trainers. A good instructor knows his material so well that all his attention goes towards making the student and dog team feel at ease. There is a very definite place for humor in teaching obedience, and a qualified instructor is relaxed and comfortable enough to see the humorous side of training dogs. Laughter eases the stress of learning.

9

Thereby Hangs a Tale

LEARNING IS STRESSFUL! (Of course, it has been said that teaching is worse!) Any time you have been placed in a learning situation, you have felt tension which comes from concentration and an inner need to succeed. Chances are when you were studying for an exam you had a serious, pensive, almost pained expression on your face. Your body was often stiffened, and you may have even looked withdrawn. Learning is hard work and is not always fun. Having learned, however, is rewarding and satisfying.

No matter how you try to sugar-coat obedience training, learning for a dog is stressful. It is important that you, as a trainer, understand that every dog is going to, at some time, go through periods of tension and stress as he learns new exercises. It is not at all uncommon for dogs to avoid the collar and leash or to run to their crates at some stressful point in their training. Of course, if the dog is still showing avoidance after he is fully trained, I would reevaluate your training methods.

Everyone wants their dogs to perform obedience happily, but you cannot become obsessed with the position of the dog's tail. It is not normal for a dog to have his ears perked and his tail high when he is concentrating or feeling stressed by a new learning situation. Should you be expected to study hard for an exam with a constant smile on your face?

There are procedures you can follow to help keep the stress of learning to a minimum. Frequent brief sessions which incorporate lots of play and praise will ease the tension. Do not become overly concerned if your dog's tail temporarily goes down while he works at thinking out a problem. If you are fair and honest in your training, his carefree, happy-go-lucky attitude will return once he understands and is confident with the new exercises. Stress cannot be avoided, but a trainer should always be aware of how much stress the dog is exhibiting and stop training before it reaches a point where the dog cannot think.

Early signs of stress include a "tongue flick," ears plastered to the dog's head, tail tucked, salivating, licking lips, panting, even a groveling, creeping posture. A common stress signal is the dog who submissively

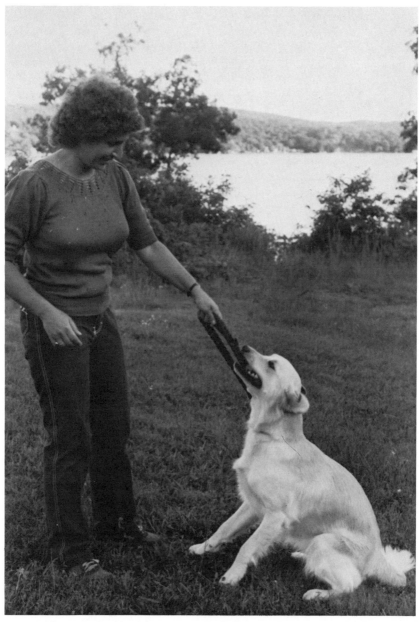

Stress can be released with brief play periods. When used properly, the leash can become an object of play. This is convenient since there is usually a leash available during training.   *Julia Brown*

raises one foot in the air as if to say, "I can't possibly do this, it's too difficult!" Individual dogs have been known to cough, yawn, wheeze, shake, sneeze, or even scratch when feeling stressed. It is important that you learn to read the signs of stress for your dog.

Dogs deal with stress in different ways. Extreme anxiety can be paralyzing as in the case of a dog who is so anxious about jumping that he will not pass the jumps to do a Go Out. The dog knows that if he does the Go Out, the jumping follows. Another example is the dog who is so anxious about the Drop-On-Recall that he will not even come when called.

Dogs, not unlike people, develop defense mechanisms to handle anxiety. Avoidance and substitution, both anxiety-reducing defense systems, are frequently evident in training. A dog who finds retrieving stressful may avoid making eye contact with where the dumbbell lands, as if to say, "If I don't see it, it isn't there, so I don't have to retrieve it." Similar avoidance is noticeable when first teaching hand signals. The dog who intentionally turns his head away as soon as you leave him on the Stand may be exhibiting avoidance of having to deal with the stress of learning signals. The good trainer will be able to make the distinction in this case between avoidance and distraction.

A substitution process is demonstrated by the dog who is perhaps anxious about doing articles and when sent to the article pile does a Go Out instead. Confusion or avoidance of anxiety? By allowing the dog to make the mistake of passing the article pile and go to the Go Out point, and by observing the dog's body language, the thinking trainer will know why the dog is not doing articles.

Since we know that dogs are stressed while learning, it makes sense to teach the dog all of the obedience exercises in Novice, Open and Utility before beginning the dog's show career. Once his show career starts, you want to avoid the pressures of learning new things. The beauty of a training method that allows a dog to think is that since the dog understands what he is doing and is not pattern-trained, he will not confuse the various exercises. I have taken my dogs to matches and shown (for exhibition) in Novice, Open and Utility, in all different orders, in one day without a single non-qualifying score (NQ). Imagine your security as a handler in the Novice ring knowing your dog can do Open and Utility! Imagine how polished your dog will look compared to the other dogs who barely know Novice and are in the midst of learning Open!

10

Why Not "NO!"

YES, YOU CAN TRAIN A DOG successfully without the word "NO." With my dogs, and in my classes, I have elected to totally remove the command "NO!" from our methods of training dogs. The reason for this is simply that most pet owners cannot say "NO!" without sounding angry. There is no place for anger in training dogs. Anger is an emotion dogs cannot understand and they either fear it or learn to ignore it. By the time most students come into class they have already used "NO!" to mean stop barking, don't bite, don't steal socks, don't jump, don't go to the bathroom in the house, and since they have rarely enforced the command, the dogs have learned to tune it out. I have seen dogs look at their owners who are screaming "NO!" as if to say, "My owner is having a temper tantrum. She will get over it shortly."

I have substituted the sound "Anh" (which sounds like you have a stomach ache and which is called "the Jewish seagull"). I have yet to find a person who can say "Anh" angrily, and the dogs soon learn that it simply means "stop what you are doing." Along with "Anh," the students are taught how to enforce the command by physically stopping the action. For household obedience problems like mouthing or stealing garbage, I prefer to stop the action physically and then praise the dog verbally. The emphasis is on the positive, not the negative. After all, we want the dog to focus on what is right. We accomplish this by not emphasizing the negative (simply stopping the bad behavior) and then praising profusely the positive.

There is nothing wrong with the word "no" as long as you are not saying it with undertones of threat. I prefer not to use any form of verbal harshness in training. It has always seemed ridiculous to me to hear a person turn to his dog and say "Bad dog! Shame on you!" as if a dog could really feel shame. Have you ever seen a dog blush? Besides, the dog is not bad, he is only wrong and I have already discussed why it is "wonderful to be wrong."

All training corrections given to a dog should be physical. The only thing he should ever hear from your voice is how wonderful he is for trying or for succeeding. This approach gives the dog security and a positive attitude. The dog never fears that you are rejecting *him* but understands that there are certain actions of which you do not approve. Your positive, happy, encouraging voice immediately following all physical corrections keeps the dog willing to try. An example: if your boss told you that you should be ashamed of a letter you wrote for him, you might take it personally and feel very low. If, on the other hand, your boss told you that you were a wonderful secretary but that you had made a number of mistakes on a letter that needed correcting, you would be more willing to continue to work for this person. While most dogs are extremely sensitive to voice, they can easily accept unemotional physical corrections when followed with praise.

By the time most people say "NO," it's too late. Have you seen the person who pushes the dog off the couch and then yells "NO"? By the time the dog hears "NO," he is off the couch and has now been corrected for doing the right thing. I prefer to physically remove the dog from the couch (stop the bad behavior) and then praise the dog verbally. Forget about "NO." You really don't need it!

While verbal harshness hinders training, it can be effective if you are intentionally trying to intimidate a dog. For example, if a dog is about to attack you—by all means, yell "NO!"

11

Understanding Corrections vs. Help

A CORRECTION is something a dog chooses to avoid. Help is an aid to the dog. Knowing when to use which can make a big difference in your training.

There are really only four distinct reasons why a dog does not respond to a command. He is either confused, afraid, distracted or feels he has a choice. If the dog is confused or afraid, I prefer to help him rather than correct him. This is the time to simplify the exercise, encourage the dog, perhaps explain it to him by using body English. If the dog is distracted or feels he has a choice, he deserves a correction such as a lead snap or jerk.

For example, a dog is learning the broad jump. He has done hundreds of jumps with his owner running with him and then jumping towards his owner. However, every time the owner attempts to stand at the side of the jump, the dog goes directly to him rather than over the jump. Does this dog deserve to be *corrected?* I think not. The dog is exhibiting confusion. The owner has neglected to teach the dog where to focus his eyes before jumping. The trainer has moved too quickly in training and the dog has missed an important point. If the dog is now corrected for the trainer's mistake, what does this do to the trust, the bond, the teamwork needed to produce top performance?

If, on the other hand, this same dog (after he has successfully done the broad jump numerous times with his owner standing at the side of the jump) is not performing because he is distracted by a pretty little bitch across the room, should he be corrected? You bet! How you correct depends on how you taught the exercise and is really not the important part of this example. As a general rule of thumb, if your dog is confused or afraid, you help him, and when he is distracted or feels he has a choice, you correct him.

How do you know when your dog is confused and when he feels he has a choice? This, my friends, is what makes one person a better trainer than another. It is called "reading a dog," and when you learn to read canine body English, you are on your way to becoming a very good trainer. You can learn to read canine body English if you are willing to spend the time. Observing dogs is probably the best way to realize that ears, eyes, head and tail carriage and overall stance of a dog reveal what he is thinking. Working with a trainer who is proficient at "reading dogs" is how most of us develop this ability.

When one of my students says to me, "My dog did _____. What is the correction?" my answer is always another question, "Why did he make the mistake and why are you so sure he is deserving of a correction?" When you are not sure why a dog did or did not perform, it is always safe to give the dog the benefit and assume he was confused or afraid. You will never do any harm by trying to help the dog before resorting to corrections. But then again, if the dog knows what you want and is choosing not to obey or if he is distracted, helping him will not solve the problem. Relax, there is always time to correct.

How do you know when your evaluation of why the dog was not performing is wrong? When your approach makes the problem worse. The dog may not even try or may attempt to run away from the entire situation. Knowing *when* to correct a dog can be more important than knowing *how* to correct him.

Reasons a Dog Does Not Obey	*Method of Correction*
	NO HARSH CORRECTIONS!
Dog is confused.	Set up a situation where dog cannot make a mistake.
	Lots of praise when dog succeeds.
Dog is afraid.	Break exercise down into simple steps. Repetition!
Dog is distracted.	Set up distracting situation and correct with lead.
	Proof the exercise.
Dog feels he has a choice.	Set up situation where dog *will* make the mistake and correct.
	Repetition in unique situations.

A phrase that repeatedly upsets me is, "He knows better, he's done it right many times before." Folks, things are not always as they appear. Four years ago I took my new Utility dog out into the back yard for a simple practice session. Since she had just finished her Utility degree, we were learning nothing new. I decided to begin with a long, happy, simple recall, and left my dog sitting contentedly as I walked 50 feet away. I turned to face her, and with a beaming smile and a clear, happy voice, I commanded, "Charo, COME." She stared straight at me and sat there! I was in shock! My Utility dog was not coming when I called her!

I regained my composure and decided to give her the benefit of the doubt (perhaps she didn't hear me because of the wind) and called her again. Again I smiled and in a loud, crisp, happy tone I called, "Charo, COME." She flinched slightly but held her sitting position.

Now at this point a pattern trainer probably would have been marching in to correct or snap a long line on the dog, but *I* knew better. I had to know *why* the dog was not responding before I would know how or if I should correct her. I ruled out fear because the dog's body English did not show any form of cowering or submission. Distraction was not the problem, either, because there was nothing going on and she was intently watching me. That left me with confusion or feeling she had a choice. While you would think it unlikely for a Utility dog to be confused on recall, it was also very unlike Charo to refuse to do something because she felt she had a choice not to.

Still at a loss, I decided to walk over to where she was still sitting and look at things from her point of view. I did not get five feet from her when I realized what was wrong. She was sitting at the "Go Out" spot and my Utility jumps were both still set up! We had spent so much time doing Directed Jumping (where the dog is not permitted to go directly to its owner between the jumps) that Charo was confused. She was waiting for a jump signal and didn't think that coming to me between the jumps was permitted. Once I knew the confusion, the answer was obvious. I would help her. I slowly walked up to her and gently guided her to me between the jumps and praised her all the way. I then repeated the exercise. This time when I commanded, "Charo, COME!" she flew to me, relieved that it was permissible to come in between the jumps. Would the correction or long line have worked? I'm sure it would have, but what would have been the long-term effect of correcting (punishing) a dog who was confused? You guessed it, panic and fear!

The recall problem might have been fixed with a correction, but at what long-term expense? By working to understand Charo's problem, the training relationship was strengthened and the problem resolved with no apprehension that might appear later in another aspect of training.

Later in this book a compulsive retrieve is explained. The trainer learns how to teach a dog that if he chooses not to retrieve, he will be corrected. Please keep in mind that not *all* refusals to retrieve are corrected. The dog is only corrected if he is refusing to retrieve because he feels he has a choice or if he is distracted.

12

Praise

PRAISE is one of the few things in life that has not yet been taxed, so by all means USE IT! I have never understood why people are stingy with praise, as if there is a limited source. You can never over-praise, provided you praise at the right time.

To each dog, praise is different. Some dogs will wag their tails if you say the right words in the right tone. For other dogs, physical contact in the form of stroking or patting will bring a joyful response. Anything that builds a dog's ego is considered praise. It is absolutely critical that you discover what words and gestures bring a tail wag from your dog if you are to train him to work happily.

Whenever possible in early training, refrain from using physical contact for praise. Too often the dog does the right thing and the owner pets the dog, which gets the dog so excited that he then does the wrong thing, e.g. break a Sit command. The dog becomes so distracted by the praise that he forgets what he did that was so great.

There are different degrees of praise. Your vocabulary may vary, but the idea is that as training progresses, so does the praise. For example, a dog does a Sit Stay with no distractions and is praised:"Good dog!" When the dog does a longer Sit Stay, he might be "Very good!" As the dog works to avoid distractions on a Sit Stay, he might be "Super" or "Great kid." Exceptional accomplishments may warrant a "Terrific" or "Excellent." If everything done well brings a simple "Good dog," why should the dog try harder?

Do not take your dog for granted. Praise all desired responses, even a simple, casual Sit that was only intended to set the dog up for the next exercise.

Dogs must be taught to accept praise without becoming crazy about it. (No, you cannot omit the praise to avoid the "crazies.") Command your dog to Sit. Now turn to him and tell him how wonderful he is, how he is the best dog ever. Use a very high, happy tone. His tail should start to wag, which is fine, but if he gets up, gently put him back into the Sit and say nothing! Keep praising. If the dog continues to move from the excitement of the praise, reposition him less gently, say nothing, and continue to praise.

It is important that the dog understands the difference between praise and release. In advanced training, you will want to praise him while he is away from you (for example, on a drop from Drop-On-Recall). If he gets up every time you praise him, you can't accomplish the exercise. If you find that you withhold praise at certain times in training because you fear the dog will get so excited he will break the exercise, stop avoiding a problem and go back and teach the dog to accept praise. It will be worth your while. You cannot have happy working dogs if your ability to praise is limited.

If you are planning to use praise (building the dog's ego) as a positive reinforcer, you must learn to reserve it for the purpose of training. There are people who cannot walk past their dogs in the house without petting them and/or praising them for simply being alive. If your dog is going to receive your approval for doing nothing, then why should he obey commands to earn praise? An ideal training situation would be one in which the dog was confined to a run or crate away from the trainer for a period of from two to four hours before each training session. The dog would then look forward to training for a chance to exercise and receive attention from his person. After training, the dog can then return to a normal family environment. I do not believe that "good obedience dogs" need to live outside so they will appreciate attention. On the other hand, praise for doing nothing breaks down a dog's motivation to perform.

A dog should be rewarded for having a good, willing attitude to try new exercises as well as for the perfect completion of an exercise. Here again degrees of praise are important. For example, a dog's first attempt at doing scent discrimination in a new surrounding may be clumsy at best. He may have hesitated in going out to the articles. His insecurity may have caused him to move slowly and tentatively toward the pile. While scenting, he may have been briefly distracted or stress may have caused him to hesitate. All of these represent imperfections which we work to correct before showing the dog, but for the moment, he finds the correct article and gathers the courage to return with it. This task, which the dog found very stressful, is deserving of great praise. The attempt and the courage, not the mechanics of the exercise, are what should be praised.

Most of the point-losing errors made by the dog in this case will correct themselves as the dog gains confidence, but such is not always the case. It is the better trainer who reads his dog and knows when effort alone is praiseworthy and when the dog is not working to his capacity.

This "praising an attempt" is difficult for some very experienced trainers to swallow. It is almost as if the more you know, the harder it gets to see point-costing errors and not fix them immediately in a new dog. But the fact remains that you cannot fix everything at once, and if you point out too many mistakes to the dog first learning, he throws up his paws as if to

Praise a dog for a straight sit by placing your left hand on his chest. By petting the dog's head into your leg, as is being done with the Irish Setter in the picture, you unintentionally teach the dog to lean on your leg.

Ron Reagan

say, "I give up! This is just too difficult for my poor little canine brain!"

Accomplished dog trainers, people who have trained one or more O.T. Chs. or even multiple U.D.s (in which category I must include myself), need to very careful. It is only by consciously disciplining ourselves that we can avoid the traps of expertise.

Have you ever noticed that each successive dog you train learns Novice through Utility in less time? As you become a more confident, experienced trainer, you demand more from a dog and you demand it sooner. As we grow as trainers the quality of dogs we train must improve to withstand the pressure of being trained by someone who "knows what he's doing."

It is sometimes helpful to record the day you begin to teach a new exercise to your dog. This way, when you feel like it is taking forever for the new dog to learn the broad jump, you can refer to your notes and realize that "forever" is actually six weeks.

Experienced trainers are not necessarily harsher. In fact, the longer I train, the less force I find it necessary to use, but the dog is nonetheless pressured by my confident demands and proficiency. Since I am no longer the awkward, klutzy handler with two left feet, the dog is expected to be able to perform smoothly as well.

Most new, promising Novice dogs are sensitive and willing. Let us not destroy these qualities by withholding praise because we see the imperfections so vividly. So what if a slightly crooked sit goes uncorrected in the beginning? Was it fast? Is he attentive? If yes, be sure to praise him! The "polish of perfection" may be added after the dog masters the major part of the exercises.

13

Training Equipment

EACH DOG IS AN INDIVIDUAL and the choice of training equipment should be based on each dog's personality, coat, previous life experiences and his handler's abilities. For example, a dog who has been tied out on a choke chain collar is likely to have built up a tolerance to the choking sensation and will probably need a different kind of collar for training. The basic rule of thumb is that we want to apply as little force as is necessary to elicit a desired response from the dog. No one collar or leash is the best choice for every dog.

If I am using a flexible lead, I prefer to train with leather. The widest leather leash the trainer can comfortably handle works best. Some people feel that it is impressive to train a 90-pound German Shorthair (for example) on a ¼″ piece of leather that I refer to as "spaghetti." Not only is it not impressive, but the handler will work much harder to achieve desired results than if he had a wider lead. It would be like trying to cut a lawn with a pair of scissors as opposed to a lawn mower!

The reason behind using the wider lead is as follows. You, the trainer, give a dog a correction by snapping or jerking the leash. This correction must then travel to the dog. The less the correction is dissipated in travel, the more correction the dog receives. Imagine, if you will, a broom stick between you and the dog. As soon as you pull your end of the stick, the dog moves because the solid wood has no "give" to it. Now look at the opposite extreme. If you hold one end of an elastic string and the dog is attached to the other end, how much is the dog affected by you pulling on your end of the string? Very little because the elastic string has so much "give" that your motion at one end is barely reaching the other end. This same principle, when applied to leashes and training, demonstrates that the denser the material between you and the dog, the faster and stronger the dog will feel a jerk.

In recent years many trainers have started using braided leashes. Since a braided leash is another way of putting more leather between you and the dog, the braided leash has proven very effective and is growing in popularity.

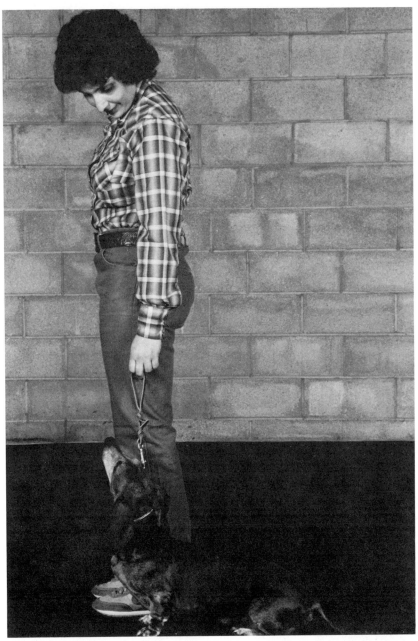

Use a handle to avoid excess leash that might allow a dog to lag or forge ahead.   *Ron Reagan*

Use the solid lead and back scratcher to position the small dog into a straight sit.　*Ron Reagan*

Train with a 3-foot leash! For years trainers have recommended a 6-foot training leash, but now we see little reason for burdening a handler with six feet of leash when 90% of the time (except for Stays) he uses only two feet of leash. Besides, if you only give a beginning handler a 3-foot leash, how far will the dog ever be able to lag or forge?

For toy breeds and dogs of similar size, train with a solid lead and a back scratcher, otherwise known as an "arm extender." The solid lead allows you to hold the dog in position without looming over him, and corrections, when needed, are given at the dog's eye level without any warning that they are coming. The back scratcher allows you the freedom to position your dog without bending. In addition to the back problems a trainer of small dogs faces, every time you bend down to the dog, you are projecting that a correction is coming and changing your position. Back scratchers praise and pet as well as position and correct.

There are many alternatives when it comes to training collars. For young puppies, small dogs or extremely sensitive dogs, start with a buckle collar. For the small dogs, a rolled leather collar works best, and for the larger breeds I like a wide nylon buckle collar. As long as you get the desired response when you snap a leash attached to a buckle collar, why go to anything more severe? I know of many O.T. Ch. small dogs that have been entirely trained on buckle collars.

When more of a response is needed, go to a small-linked choke chain collar that releases easily. The collar should fit so that when pulled snug there is not more than two inches of chain before you attached the leash. I usually tell my students (who always fear that the collar is too tight) that you want the smallest collar you can get over the dog's head. For dogs with very large heads and smaller necks, you can buy a chain collar that you put on with a buckle or snap. Since this collar does not slide over the head, you can get the proper fit. The collar should be put on so that the part that attaches to the end of your lead comes from on top of the dog's neck.

When the choke chain or slip chain collar is not effective, the next step is a prong collar (also called a "pinch collar" or a "German collar"). The prong collar is a valuable training tool when used properly. Unfortunately, this collar looks like some sort of medieval torture, and the uneducated owner is often afraid of it. The prong collar should fit snugly around the dog's neck, up high and behind the ears. The individual prongs come apart to fit the collar as well as to adjust the size of the collar. Since when worn properly the collar does not slide, put the collar on the dog so that the part that attaches to the leash is on the right side of the dog's neck.

The prong collar works on an entirely different principle than the choke collar. It is designed to pinch skin evenly all around the neck. Since the prongs are dull, no harm is done to the dog's skin. By distributing the correction all around the dog's neck (instead of in one place as with the choke collar), less force is needed on the leash to impress the dog. The

The correct way to put on a slip chain collar. Notice the small smooth links that slide easily as the collar is tightened and then released   *Ron Reagan*

This collar is on incorrectly and will not release easily. Notice the use of the braided leash.
Julia Brown

The prong collar is positioned on the dog's neck so that the part that attaches to the leash is on the right side of the dog's neck. *Ron Reagan*

The prong collar fits snugly, directly behind the dog's ears.   *Ron Reagan*

Step one in removing the prong collar is to squeeze an individual link as you slide an adjoining link up and out of the collar. *Ron Reagan*

To apply or remove the prong collar any two links are separated. *Ron Reagan*

prong collar is particularly effective on dogs who are immune to being choked because they have been tied on choke collars or permitted to pull on choke collars for months. There are other dogs who, for whatever reason, cannot tolerate a choking sensation and panic, gag and cough when pressure from a simple choke chain collar is applied to their necks. These dogs tolerate the pinch from the prong collar very well. I once owned a Border Collie who had been snapped so hard on a choke chain as a puppy that her throat was damaged. The slightest pressure on her trachea from a chain sent her into a gagging fit. Luckily, she had no problem tolerating a small prong collar.

It is preferable to see large, heavy dogs who may lunge on a prong collar because you will never harm a dog with a prong collar. A large, heavy dog lunging on a choke collar, where all the pressure is at one point, could damage his trachea. The prong collar is also preferred when you are trying to preserve a dog's coat. The chain and nylon choke collars will break and rip out the hair on the neck. When a dog comes into class with all of the hair on one side of his neck worn off, this is a candidate for a prong collar!

Prong collars come in three sizes of links, termed small, medium and large. I have never had to use the large size and don't recommend it because the links are too stiff to open and close easily.

We often refer to the prong collar as "power steering" since you need less force to give an effective correction. Small people with large dogs welcome this advantage!

A prong collar should not be used in the case of an aggressive dog who may bite. You cannot successfully hang a dog on a prong collar when trying to keep him from getting close enough to bite you. With aggressive dogs that are too strong to control on a choke collar, use both collars and two leashes. If the dog lunges, restrain with the prong collar. Then if he goes to bite, hang him with the choke collar.

The only problem trainers ever have with using the prong collar is that people fear what looks horrible and what they don't understand. Because of this understandable apprehension, it helps to put a prong collar on the owner's arm or leg first and snap it so that they experience what the dog will feel. So far I have yet to have any owner scream in pain from being corrected with a prong collar. In fact, when compared to the snap from a choke chain collar, owners prefer the prong collar. It is important that you explain to owners that their dogs might yelp when this collar is first used but that this is because they are surprised by the new feeling and they are capable of verbalizing as the collar is not choking them. Since the prong collar is used less harshly and less frequently to control a dog, it is often much kinder than the choke chain collar.

If you notice the absence of the nylon choke collar from my writing, it is because I have never been happy with the results from a nylon choke collar. Nylon collars do not release quickly and often get tangled in long hair. Part of the effectiveness of the choke chain is the sound it makes when snapped. This sound helps to sharpen the dog's response. I do not see how the nylon choke is considered to be a milder collar than the choke chain since the end result of both is a choking sensation! Perhaps people feel less abusive if they can't hear the sound of the chain?

An instructor once explained that she didn't allow chain collars in her classes because the sound of the chain bothered some dogs. My feeling is that if your dog is afraid of the sound of a chain collar, you would be a lot wiser to get him over this fear than to try to avoid these sounds for the rest of his life. Other than being less likely to break, I see no advantage to using a nylon vs. a chain choke collar.

Any piece of training equipment is only effective and unabusive when used properly and applied to the right dog. There is nothing that prohibits you from using different collars on the same dog for different problems. Some of my dogs only feel a prong collar once in their lives, and that's when they need motivation to move faster on the outside circle of a Figure 8!

A good trainer is an open-minded, flexible person who reacts to the individual dog and to a moment in his training.

14

Choosing and Raising the Future O.T. Ch.

PUPPY TESTING to find the "good obedience dogs" is the current fad. While I have no doubt that you can test puppies to predict their future personality, keep in mind that any test is only as valid as the person performing the test and evaluating the results. If you are not experienced with testing puppies, you would probably be better off trusting the judgment of a reputable breeder who is involved with showing and training for obedience.

Keep in mind that the great obedience dogs of the past, present and future are really great dog-and-handler *teams*. It is the combination of dog and handler personalities that leads to O.T. Chs. What might be the perfect obedience prospect for one person might be a reject in the hands of another. Analyze yourself and your training style. Are your needs better met with a dominant dog, very resilient to bouncing back after a correction, or does your personality blend better with an outgoing, sensitive sweetheart? Good breeders know their puppies and can help find the best prospect *for you.*

Can you breed O.T. Chs.? I believe you can, but two O.T. Ch. dogs bred together do not necessarily produce top obedience prospects. Certain lines do seem to carry more genes which produce driving (energetic), willing dogs with the structure to sit squarely and jump easily.

When choosing a puppy for obedience, look for the pup that chooses to make eye contact, the people-oriented puppy who willingly follows you. You want the puppy who is outgoing, friendly, inquisitive, energetic and likes to show off—a "group winner."

Taking a puppy home at seven weeks seems to be the preferred age as documented by laboratory tests which indicate that the eighth through eleventh weeks begin a critical period where the puppy should experience no trauma.

What often makes the difference between a good dog and a great dog is early socialization. Take the puppy (inoculated, of course) everywhere! Visit friends, go shopping, audit training classes, spectate at matches, stay in hotel rooms! The more people, dogs, sights and sounds you expose your puppy to early on in life, the easier it will be to demand attention from him later in training and the more secure he will be.

Teach your puppy to play. Games of retrieve, tug of war (alternate who wins), hide and seek and tag help develop a relationship between you and the dog and later on will serve as a release from the stress of learning. Pups should have the opportunity to play with metal objects in preparation for scent articles.

Quiet times alone with your puppy are also important. Take walks (on leash) in the woods, sit together in the sun and take time to stroke and talk to your puppy. This helps him understand your tones of voice and builds a bond between you two which will grow into a working team. Whenever possible, make eye contact.

Be fair and honest with your pup. Never put him in uncomfortable situations, for example with young children who might hurt or tease him. You want your dog to trust that you will protect him. Never do anything to jeopardize this trust. Later on he must trust that if you command him to Stay or Jump that it is safe to do so.

If you want your dog to respect you, begin by respecting him. Respond to his affection. Be alert to his needs, i.e. meal time, grooming and housebreaking. Make sure to take a lot of time from your schedule to spend alone with your puppy.

Your pup will learn to be handled and will appreciate your attention if you groom him regularly. Learn to clean ears and teeth and to cut his nails and care for his coat. Admiration and love grow on a grooming table!

While time spent with your puppy is important, be careful not to make him overly dependent. There should be time during the day for the puppy to be by himself, either in a pen or crate. This helps the dog develop independence. As the pup gets a little older, occasionally hand his leash to a responsible person from time to time and walk away. Dogs who are never left when they are young may have anxiety to overcome on out-of-sight Stays later on in training.

In preparation for straight fronts, always greet your dog from in front and pet him towards you and evenly on both sides of his face as you encourage eye contact. Petting a dog on his side causes the dog to turn his side to you, which is not desired in obedience. When feeding your dog his daily meal, talk to him just before you put his food down in front of him. The bowl of food draws the pup's eyes up to your face, so take advantage of the attention.

Whenever possible, pet your dog under his chin and towards you, which will encourage him to lift his head. Handle your dog from his head to his toes to his tail. Your pup should be comfortable with being handled all over in preparation for the Stand for Examination.

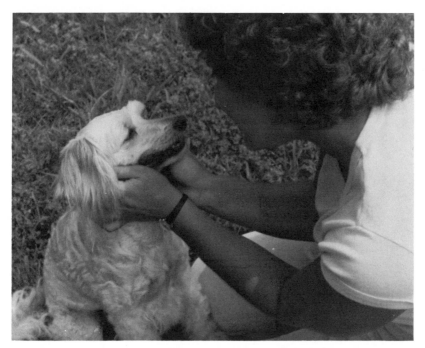

Encourage eye contact by pleasantly looking directly into the dog's eyes while gently holding the dog's head. *Julia Brown*

Occasionally "rough house" with your pup. Some loving rough handling will help him to learn to accept corrections later in training.

Never put a choke collar (nylon or chain) on your pup until absolutely necessary. (See Chapter 13 - *Training Equipment*.)

Your dog's health is your responsibility. A healthy dog trains easier and performs better. Keep your pup free of internal and external parasites, lean, well muscled and free of mats and excess hair. If you have a hairy breed, work to keep his eyes clean so he can maintain eye contact. Short nails help a dog jump easier and move more freely. A clean, brushed coat never hurt any dog's score in the obedience ring!

Building a bond with your puppy is setting a strong foundation on which to build a good training relationship. The end result is a dog and handler team who work like they belong together.

Training should be incorporated into a puppy's life in a natural way. It is impossible to state an age at which formal training should begin. Smaller breeds tend to mature faster physically and are thus able to handle the physical demands of training (e.g. sitting squarely) at an earlier age. In general, smaller dogs can be started younger.

From the moment you get your puppy, attention should be encouraged and praised but not demanded until such time as you begin a formal training program.

Young puppies (3-6 months) can and should learn to Sit, Down, Stand and Come on command, taught gently and carefully. (In the case of a large breed puppy who will not yet sit up straight on his haunches, omit the Sit until such time as he is physically capable of doing it.) "Come" at this point is done randomly, from wherever the pup is standing, and there is no sit front required.

Heeling and Stays are best left until the dog is older (6-12 months). While a puppy can learn to walk next to you attentively, it is of little value to attempt to teach him foot cues or rhythm since as he grows his stride will change and his ability to concentrate is limited. Stays require extreme discipline for some overzealous obedience prospects, and to ask a young pup to sit perfectly still is often more than he can emotionally handle. So, wait a few months until he has some of the "ants out of his pants." In early training, the only truly important thing you need to accomplish is teaching the dog to pay attention to you! Once you have his attention, the rest will fall into place.

To be most effective, a trainer should be aware of the various growth stages a dog is likely to experience. Much has already been written about "critical periods" in a dog's life. How these periods affect a dog's ability to learn can be most enlightening. In the book, *Training Your Dog, The Step-by-Step Manual* by Joachim Volhard and Gail Tamases Fisher, critical periods are defined to be:

Birth to Seven Weeks (0-49 days)
Socialization Period (7-12 weeks)
Fear Imprint Period (8-11 weeks)
Seniority Classification Period (12-16 weeks)
Flight Instinct Period (4-8 months)
Second Fear Imprint Period (6-14 months)
Maturity (1-4 years)

While much has been written about young puppies, I am particularly interested in a period of a dog's life that I refer to as Adolescence (13-24 months) and Pre-adolescence (9-13 months) for it is during this time that dogs receive most of their formal training in preparation for a show career. While each dog and breed of dog must be considered an individual, you cannot help but see recurring patterns as you continue to raise and train dogs in obedience.

The adolescent dog has two paws in adulthood and two paws in puppyhood. While at times he appears calm and secure, there are other times when, if left unsupervised, he will have a "pillow party." (That's where you come home after a brief jaunt to find that it has snowed pillow stuffing all over your house!) Your young, aspiring show dog is once again returned to his crate whenever you need to depart.

Erratic behavior, such as running away and not coming when called one day (even in a dog who has been trained to come) and then clinging to mommy or daddy the next day, is not uncommon. I have heard trainers say, "He was such a socialized puppy. We did all the good things like walking him through town and banging on shopping carts, and now at 10 months he's spooking at a garbage dumpster!" This is not at all unusual as Volhard and Fisher describe in their "Second Fear Imprint Period, 6-14 months."

Astute trainers may also notice a difficulty to concentrate and that the adolescent dog is more easily distracted and almost "spacey." At a time in their lives when sexual thoughts dance in their heads, and other dogs seem much more important, we as trainers are concerned with Figure Eights! Gawky, distracted, bodies changing, often overly energetic, the adolescent dog is not always in the best frame of mind to learn. Not yet sure of who he is or where he fits in, the confused 9-24 months old can find training too stressful to enjoy. Parents report horror stories about raising teenagers, and dog owners rant and rave about their 1½ year old dog who looks mature but is still undisciplined and unpredictable.

In my experience with large breeds, two seems to be the magic age where the dog finally starts working with you instead of against you. It is also around two that the dog exhibits a certain "presence" when exhibited in the obedience ring, as if to say, "Look at me! I know who I am and what I'm doing!" I like to show dogs in Novice right around two years of age.

A good trainer is concerned with the dog at the end of the leash—his mental and physical status. We can only teach as much as our student is ready to learn. This learning rate will change throughout the dog's developmental stages. More than once I have doubted the potential of a dog I was training when the dog was about a year and a half old. Experience has taught me to reserve judgment until after 24 months.

As puppies grow up, they might reach a stage where training is not a pleasant experience and the pup appears disinterested. There is nothing wrong with interrupting the training process for a month or more until the dog is again receptive. The ideal trainer trains instinctively, giving the dog as much as he can handle while at the same time watching for signs of stress and then removing the pressure. There must not be a rush if your goal is a top dog-and-handler *team*.

15

Anticipation

ANTICIPATION, when the dog does something before he's told to, is a predictable stage of learning. Many obedience exercises as we know them are nothing more than a series of anticipations which we allow. On the Retrieve-Over-the-High-Jump exercise, we give the dog a single command to jump. He then anticipates that we will ask him to pick up the dumbbell, return over the jump and sit front. He has anticipated three commands. It is easy to see why dogs go directly to heel position in anticipation of the next command.

In the learning stages, anticipation should be permitted, and with some insecure dogs, encouraged. However, once the dog understands the exercise, improper anticipation must be stopped. Since most anticipation is caused by confusion, help the dog understand rather than correct him for being confused.

If a dog is anticipating a Recall or any exercise where he is *coming to you,* put him on leash and hand the leash to someone standing behind the dog. When the dog gets up, the leash holder gently repositions the dog while saying nothing. When the dog is called, the person holding the leash simply drops it. The dog will eventually realize that he should not come until called.

If the dog is anticipating a Retrieve, or any exercise where he is *going away from you,* put a 6-foot leash on the dog and drop it on the floor. Step on the leash with your left foot. Now do everything you can to encourage the dog to anticipate. Use his name as if you were going to command him to "TAKE IT," flinch your body with sharp movements, lean forward, etc. When the dog anticipates, say nothing. He will be stopped by your weight on the leash. After he gets caught, reposition him gently and begin again as if nothing happened. Remember, *do NOT correct* confusion. When you finally do send the dog, simply lift your weight off the leash. This method is more effective than holding the dog by the collar because the dog never knows when you are standing on the leash and he is forced to *think* about what you say, that allows him to retrieve.

If a dog anticipates the Finish, sit him in front of you on leash.

Command his name, flinch, do everything you can to cause him to anticipate, then gently stop him with the leash. He will soon understand that he is only to move on the finish command.

For anticipation of the Drop-On-Recall, see Chapter 34.

For anticipated signals on the Signal exercise, allow more time between the signals to help cause the anticipation. Then, when the dog anticipates, give him a verbal command (not a threatening shout) for what he should be doing. By practicing signals out of order, you will also counteract the anticipation.

Certain breeds of dogs are more prone to anticipation than others. If you are training one of these breeds, e.g. Border Collies, Poodles, some Golden Retrievers, allow the learning stage, which includes anticipation, to go on for less time than you would with another breed.

As a rule, dogs trained to listen carefully and to think about what they are doing have fewer incidents of anticipated exercises.

16

Creatures Big and Small

EACH DOG AND EACH HANDLER are individual. To attempt to train each team the same way is to be unfairly simplistic. While I certainly advocate group classes, there must be individualization within the classes if dogs are going to have an opportunity to reach potential. What may be an effective method on a dog the size of a Golden Retriever or German Shepherd is not necessarily the best choice for a dog the size of a Yorkie or Papillon. With some of our giant and toy breeds, it takes a lot of imagination to modify training methods. If you are the owner of a toy or giant breed of dog and instinctively feel that methods offered by your instructor are not appropriate for your dog, trust your instincts and don't use them!

It never ceases to amaze me that people will do things to their dogs—although they don't feel comfortable with them—simply because some well-known, winning trainer said it was the thing to do. An owner should always have the courage to take the responsibility for the specific training methods he uses on his dogs. If you do not feel comfortable with a method, don't use it! If a method makes no sense to you, don't use it, for if it doesn't make sense to you, how in the world is it going to make sense to the dog?

If we agree that each dog and handler is unique, then we must accept that each team has different physical and mental limitations. For example, each dog and each handler has a different energy level. It is not the energy level itself that is so important as it is the combination of dog and owner's energy level. For a dog to be a top performing dog, he must be teamed up with a compatible handler. A very energetic Golden in the hands of a sweet old gentleman or a very overweight lady will not fare as well as the same energetic Golden in the hands of a slim, hyper person. This does not mean that the sweet old gentleman or overweight lady will never have the ability to train a superb obedience dog, but I suggest there is a better choice of dog for them. Notice I said "dog" and not "breed." I believe you can find the right dog for you in the breed of your choice—you might have to search for a while. I have seen exceptional dogs of all breeds. At the moment I have a young lady in class with a female Saint Bernard that is as fast and agile and alert and willing and accurate as any Golden Retriever I have seen! No one will ever tell her she's a Saint Bernard.

To ask more from a dog than it is capable of giving is cruel. Not all dogs are fast by nature. To constantly correct or attempt to frighten a dog for the sake of speed in obedience is, to me, abusive. If speed for the sake of speed is what is important to you, then I recommend you buy a faster dog. Spectators watch outside the rings at obedience trials and see very fast, high scoring dogs, and for some reason they attribute this speed to how the dogs were trained. While I agree that training plays a part, I maintain that these very dogs are naturally energetic and that what training has done is channel the energy rather than create it.

Dogs and people are limited by their structure. I once owned a very limited dog. After weeks of working on straight sits, I was so exasperated one day that I decided to try an experiment. On a quiet afternoon I took my little furry friend into the living room and gently commanded, "SIT." Then, one by one I carefully positioned each foot where it should be for a perfectly straight sit. Just as I let go of the fourth paw, perfectly in position, the dog fell over! Her structure was such that it was impossible for her to sit squarely. I still loved her but gave up on the idea of ever getting her to do a straight sit.

You train each dog a little differently, and each dog you train will teach you something new about dog training. Let us understand and deal with our limitations and not ignore them. To pretend that a Great Dane can be trained the same as a Chihuahua is not logical!

If a 200 score is what you are after, then you must begin with a dog who is physically and mentally capable of perfection. Then, if you train it perfectly and you become a 200 handler, all you need is a judge who will score a 200 if he or she sees it!

17

Special Small Dog and Big Dog Techniques

TO BE SUCCESSFUL training toys or giant breeds you must be more creative than the average handler. The obedience world was not designed for the extremes. If you are choosing a dog for obedience, always look for a large toy or a small giant within the breed of your choice.

Toy dogs, while fragile, are not helpless. Refrain from carrying them all over and from over-protecting them from the real world. In early training, work with the small dog on a table and in your lap to encourage eye contact. Did you know you could start to teach heeling with the dog at your side on an oval table? Raising the dog up to table level also helps start the signal exercises. For heeling toy dogs, use the solid lead (see Chapter 13 - *Training Equipment*) and a back scratcher to correct and pet. To mark fronts and finishes, make use of 12-inch rulers as guides for the dog to line up with. If Directed Jumping is a problem, put the jumps close together and get down on your knees to give the signals. If you're having trouble keeping your toy's attention, try dangling a toy or food from a string to start your dog looking up. Lagging can be a problem as many of the toy dogs lack stamina. Rather than snapping forward with your solid lead, "goose" the little guy from behind with your back scratcher!

While the "littles" require a lot of creative, sensitive training, giant breeds are often a case of brute force. Have you ever noticed that it's always little people who buy big dogs? A common large dog problem is speed, especially on a Recall. While you might get response snapping a Golden on a longline, good luck with a Newfie! To motivate large dogs, throwing things from behind works best. While we often begin with throw chains (a circle of heavy chain) with a giant breed, we have been known to throw metal chairs (not at the dog but behind him to evoke a response) at very large, unresponsive dogs. Make sure the dog is on a longline when you use throw chains or other objects. This is to assure that the dog comes to you rather than panicking and running away from you.

Use the solid lead and back scratcher to hold the small dog in heel position so that he learns where it is.

Ron Reagan

Use the solid lead and back scratcher to teach a straight sit at heel without having to bend over, thus changing the dog's view of the handler.   *Ron Reagan*

61

Use the leash as a sling to teach the small dog the stand signal. For very sensitive dogs, padding the part of the leash that goes underneath the dog is helpful.

Ron Reagan

Use the back scratcher to teach a tight about turn to a small dog.   *Ron Reagan*

Crowding from a large dog is more than a problem, it can be hazardous to your health! Swinging your right arm across your body works for many dogs. With the giants, you might want to hold a metal dustpan and make contact with the side of the dog's face as you sweetly command "OFF." It may sound something like the "Gong Show." And, for the Drop-In-Motion exercise, instead of using your arm as the "windmill" signal, try a plastic wiffle bat! The bat makes a lot of noise but wouldn't hurt the big guy.

When it comes to training the very large and the very small dogs, the secret is to think—be imaginative! If it makes sense, try it! Do not be afraid of what others might think—you can always hand them the leash and tell them to see if they can get results the conventional way!

18

Proofing

"PROOFING" is a term used to describe a technique of testing a dog's understanding of an exercise. Proofing clarifies concepts while strengthening the dog's concentration and confidence. Every exercise you ever teach your dog to perform in obedience should be proofed before you ever consider taking him to shows. Proofing gives the owner the confidence he needs to show off his dog at a trial. When devising new ways to proof your dog, both you and the dog become inspired and challenged. It is a good way to keep from becoming bored.

There are different degrees of proofing a given exercise. That is to say, some forms of proofing are more difficult for the dog to withstand. For example, petting a dog on a Sit Stay might be easier for the dog to tolerate and remain sitting than the temptation of offering him a hamburger. Different proofs are more challenging to different dogs. The "chow hound" finds food proofs very difficult while the non-eater is hardly tempted by the food. A good trainer is aware of his dog's weaknesses (food, touch, sound, sight) and works to gradually increase the difficulty of the proof test. For example, with a noise-sensitive dog, it would not be wise to start introducing loud applause until the dog was comfortable with the noise of a single hand clap.

Examples of Proofing

Sit Stay —

Put the dog on a Sit Stay and throw balls and toys in front of him.

Have others give him alternate commands like Down and Come.

Spray him with water to simulate a rain shower.

Have him hear applause.

Take him to distracting, busy, noisy places and practice your Sit Stay.

Tempt him to move for food or other dogs.

In general, try anything other than calling his name to get him to make a mistake.

Recalls —

Leave your dog with his back to you.

Leave your dog and have someone pet him or feed him as you call him.

Call him and you disappear around a corner.

Have him go around obstacles or through people to get to you.

Stand —

Stand your dog, leave him and put slow, steady pressure against the leash. Does he resist, demonstrating an understanding of Stay? (Same is good for all Stay positions, i.e. Sit and Down.)

Step over him.

Have different kinds of people examine him. Have people examining him wear raincoats, hats, beards, umbrellas.

If possible, try crawling under him.

Stand him on various surfaces, e.g. plastic, wood, stone, wire.

Finishes —

Finish your dog and have someone behind you tempt the dog with food or toys.

Finish standing close to a wall.

Finish and just before the dog sits, make a minor move forward, backward, or sideways. Does the dog adjust?

Finish your dog from a Down position in front of you.

Heeling —

Heel in all different places with all kinds of distractions.

Have someone tempt the dog with food or toys while you are heeling.

Head towards an open door or any other distraction and do a sudden About Turn. Is the dog distracted?

Teach the dog to heel sideways and backwards.

Do 360 degree and 270 degree turns.

Practice Figure Eights at a slow pace. Alternate your Figure 8 patterns, for example two of one post and then one of another.

Turn just before you halt.

Halt facing walls and baby gates.

Practice fast to slow to fast.

Have someone play frisbee over you while you are heeling.

A Golden Retriever is being proofed on Scent Articles. If the dog is distracted by the turtles and stops working the articles, he will be corrected. This teaches the dog to focus his attention on what he is being commanded to do and to block out distractions.   *Bauman*

A Border Collie is being proofed for Hand Signals with the use of a donut. If the dog focuses his attention on the distraction, a correction for a missed signal will follow.   *Ron Reagan*

66

Retrieving —

Retrieve all different kinds of objects from all different places.

Put your dumbbell up high, under a chair, under a jacket, in a pot of water, on top of a person lying on the floor, next to another dog, next to food, under another animal, off the cage of a guinea pig, etc.

Test every possible situation until you are convinced that the dog will retrieve his dumbbell from anywhere.

Jumps —

Change location of jumps.

Change appearance of jumps, e.g. put coats, flowers, balloons on them. Simulate shadows on the jumps.

Broad Jump — Use fewer boards at the same distance to tempt a mistake.

Gloves —

Turn to a glove, give a signal, praise for looking, but don't send the dog.

Turn to one glove and send to another.

Use brown gloves which may not be as obvious on dark surfaces. (See Chapter 40 - **Directed Retrieve.**)

Articles —

Use two or more sets of articles.

Stand articles up on end.

Put some articles up on a chair or coffee table and some underneath. Alternate where the scented one is.

Have all kinds of noise distractions while your dog works the articles.

Have two dogs work the same pile of articles. (Make sure you are using a third scent on your pile of articles.)

Put food and other unscented objects out in between your articles. Is the dog distracted or does he keep working?

Go Outs —

Do them at all different distances.

Do them in different places.

Throw objects before and during to distract the dog.

Tempt him to go off center by having a person or other dog behind barrier off center.

Stop your dog short. The next time, send him past where you stopped him.

Anticipation —

You can proof all anticipation by setting up the exercise and saying the dog's name only. Help him back into position if he moves.

Say his name, followed by an extraneous command like "LISTEN" or "BANANAS." Help him if he moves.

Flinch with sudden body motions. Reposition him if he responds as if it were a command.

Proofing should be fun and imaginative. It requires that you want the dog to be wrong so that you can show him (not necessarily correct him) what right is. Remember, "wrong is wonderful!" If you can't bear to proof because you are encouraging a mistake, you will end up doing a lot less training and a lot more praying. Proofing causes and solves mistakes *before* the dog starts making them up on his own.

It is not bad to be wrong—it is only wrong. When the dog has exhausted all wrong possibilities, then and only then does he understand what right is. Trainers who do not proof are often heard to say, "My dog works great at home!" or "He never did that before." Trainers who proof cause all their mistakes in practice and get reliable performances in the ring.

As with most good techniques, anything can be taken too far or, as the cliche goes, "too much of a good thing is no good." The object of proofing is to test the dog's understanding of an exercise, not to drive him crazy!

Weak links in training should be proofed more frequently as in the case of the dog who tends to forget what he is doing on the Long Sit and lies down. It would not be excessive to proof the Long Sit just prior to doing Sits and Downs every time you show the dog. (Of course, you will have to leave the show grounds to do this as proofing is considered training.) On the other hand, if you have no problem with the Retrieve exercise, while an occasional challenge will keep the exercise interesting, there is no reason to make every single retrieve a monumental proofing test.

How extensively you proof should also depend on your dog's personality. Some dogs thrive on challenges while others are easily stressed by having to perform and, if pushed, may have a nervous breakdown. By reading the anxiety level in your dog, you will know whether to proof further or simplify an exercise.

Good training provides the dog with a balance between the confidence of knowing he can do an exercise by just doing it and the proofing which keeps him thinking about what he is doing while stretching his level of confidence. A shy Sheltie who is made to retrieve a dumbbell from next to a person's leg gains the confidence he needs to retrieve from anywhere in the ring. This same shy Sheltie need not be made to retrieve his dumbbell from next to a vicious dog as this might traumatize the Sheltie to a point where he would no longer even attempt the exercise.

68

19

Homework Counts— When It's Done Right!

BEGINNING STUDENTS are instructed to do ten minutes of homework with their dogs every day. What exactly is homework?

1. A ten-minute session, or two five-minute sessions, is really all that is required to effectively train a dog, provided the handler is making full use of the ten minutes.
2. Choose a time of the day when you are in good spirits and when your dog is awake. Don't drag him out of a sound sleep, throw the collar on and expect response. Some low-energy dogs respond better if confined to a crate four hours before practice.
3. Before you start to work, write down on a piece of paper exactly what you plan to work on. You need not practice *everything* every day. Concentrate on no more than three exercises when in the learning stages. Choose an exercise that you enjoy, an exercise the dog enjoys and then something that you both need to work on!
4. Always begin with a short (two-minute) warm-up of Heeling or play for your dog. Vary your patterns. One day you might concentrate on only right turns. Do a lot of happy talking and get him excited about what he is going to do next. Avoid any major corrections for the first few minutes of training. This allows the dog to ready his mind and body in preparation for work without the anxiety of a correction. This helps you establish a positive working attitude with the dog.
5. If you have a particular problem exercise or an exercise that the dog has just recently learned, work that exercise briefly, then do something the dog understands well, and then return to the problem exercise.
6. Do NOT become patterned. That is to say, do not work things in the same order or in the same place every time. If you did a Recall in one direction one day, do it in another direction the next.

7. Work briskly while correcting deliberately without running or diving at the dog.

8. Keep it fun! Play ball between exercises if necessary if you find the dog is not alert and motivated. If you or your dog get bored, stop and think about how you can make the exercises more challenging. (See Chapter 18 - *Proofing*.)

9. Always end each session on a positive note. The last thing the dog does should be something he does well. Always leave him with the feeling that he has succeeded. If he has done nothing well, just play a favorite game or roll on the ground to let him know that you still love him. End training before the dog is too tired to perform.

10. As the dog gains experience and you have been training for a few months, you can extend the training sessions in an effort to help the dog build stamina. Train as long as you want to but stop before the dog is too tired to learn.

20

The Fifth Week Plateau

AS A TRAINER OF DOGS, it is important for you to know as much as possible about how dogs learn.

My experience training dogs seems to suggest a distinct learning pattern. When learning a new command, dogs demonstrate progress daily for a few weeks. After approximately four weeks or 32 days, something very unusual happens. The dog acts as if he has never heard the command before! He appears confused and makes a poor, if any, attempt to respond. For the naïve trainer, this can be a devastating, depressing, not to mention frustrating experience.

Interestingly enough, whether you train the dog or not for the next few days, approximately five to ten days later the dog's memory of the desired response has returned! I have heard this phenomenon referred to as "the fifth week plateau."

There are various theories as to why this occurs. Some suggest that when a dog first learns something, the information goes into his short-term memory. It is hypothesized that when the information is in transit from short-term memory to long-term memory, the dog is unable to recall it.

Similar observations have been documented by other trainers.

Karen Pryor, in her book *Don't Shoot the Dog* (Simon & Schuster, 1984) refers to a "pre-learning dip." She explains:

> You have just shaped a behavior, and now you are bringing it under stimulus control. But just as the subject seems to be showing signs of responding to the stimulus, it suddenly not only stops responding to the stimulus, but stops responding altogether. It acts as if it had never heard of the thing you shaped it to do.

Karen Pryor has a different theory about why this strange learning behavior occurs. She writes:

> What is going on in my opinion is that at first the subject is learning a cue without really being aware of doing so; the trainer sees only a heartening tendency toward slowly increasing correct performance. But then as the subject notices the cue and becomes aware that the signal has something to do

with whether it gets reinforced. At that point it attends to the signal rather than offering the behavior.

As trainers this phenomenon helps explain some strange behavior. Any time we teach a dog something, there appears to be a period of time when he acts as if he never learned it. We can theorize why this happens, but perhaps this is not as important as simply expecting it to occur and avoiding our own frustrations.

Plateaus are easily recognized. A dog who, for example, has been going down for four weeks on command only, suddenly becomes totally bewildered, for no apparent reason, like he has never heard the word before in his life. This is a plateau. As the trainer, you should proceed as if you were first teaching the exercise.

The dog's learning process is further complicated by the fact that a dog will probably reach a plateau for every step of every exercise you ever teach him! Rather than try to keep track of which plateaus have been reached, you are better off to train through these periods and understand why the dog is not responding like he once was.

Different dogs reach plateaus at different rates. The 32 days is only an average. I have also noticed that the length of time spent at a plateau varies from dog to dog. Some dogs pass through a plateau in as little as three days, others go for as long as 14 days. There are people who observe that their dogs train better if they are not worked every day. Could it be that they miss having to deal with some of the learning plateaus?

21

The ON and OFF Switch
of Dog Attention

NO DOG OR PERSON works all of the time. For a dog to be reliable and accurate, when he is obeying a command, we must have his undivided attention. It is unrealistic to demand such concentration from a dog indefinitely, so we have created an ON and OFF switch which lets the dog know when he is working and when he is not. It is very important that the owner be aware of *when* his dog is on a command and make sure to enforce the command. I have observed handlers at a dog show turn to their dogs and say, "HEEL" and then proceed to walk leisurely to the restroom while the dog lags, sniffs and does whatever else six feet of leash will allow. Did the owner really mean "Heel?" Does "Heel" only count in the ring? How is the dog supposed to know which "Heel" is the one where you want his attention? A simple, "Fido, Let's Go" would have gotten them both to the restrooms and would have been a lot less damaging to Fido's training.

Think about what you say and only say what you mean and plan to enforce. If your dog jumps up on you, do you say "Get DOWN?" Do you really mean "DOWN" (as in ". . . on the floor"), or would "OFF" have been more appropriate? When you leave your house, do you turn to your dog and say, "Now you STAY there"? Is that the same "Stay" that you will use in the ring? How is the dog to know the difference?

The OFF switch is very easy to teach. I use the command "Okay," throw my hands up over my head, yell, cheer, play with the dog, and by golly he realizes that he's off duty. I like to teach beginners the OFF switch first because the dogs learn it so quickly and respond so positively. It helps to generate exhuberant praise which is sometimes difficult to get from beginners. Pleased with themselves for having taught their dogs the OFF switch so quickly, handlers are now very motivated to teach the ON switch. What they do not realize is that teaching a dog to pay attention and to concentrate is perhaps the most difficult task they have ahead of them.

The word "SIT" is the ON switch to let the dog know that work is beginning and it's time to pay attention. It really doesn't matter what word you use, but I have found "SIT" to be convenient when showing your dog because in every ring you ever walk into and before each exercise in Novice, Open and Utility, you are permitted to turn to your dog and say, "SIT." When "sit" also means "pay attention," you are off to a good start.

In my own classes and with my own dogs, attention is taught *before* heeling. I have yet to understand how a dog who is not paying attention can learn to heel correctly.

Before you can even attempt to get attention, you must have a dog who knows that it is possible to sit and stand (eventually heel) while looking up at his owner, and you must have a dog who has learned to accept eye contact. You can prepare a young dog for attention work by making an effort to look into your dog's eyes, stroking him under the chin and talking to him softly. Looking at his owner should be a pleasant experience for the dog. Part of your petting and grooming time should be devoted to looking into your dog's eyes. Small dogs may be in laps or on tables. Take the time to get down on the floor with your dogs and establish eye contact. Any time your dog looks up at you around the house, acknowledge him with a pleasant word or two.

Before starting formal training, try to establish a one-to-one relationship between your dog and yourself. If your dog lives outside, take the time to do these exercises with your dog as well. All potentially nasty dogs or owners who might fear putting their faces near their dogs should be handled separately and differently! You must first be dominant over your dog before you can expect to establish eye contact and demand attention. Please note that when I refer to eye contact I am talking about a smiling, friendly face. Don't stare or glare at your dog unless you want to get bitten or upset the dog. In dog language, a stare is often interpreted as a challenge.

Attention for the adult dog is started with the dog on a collar and leash, sitting next to you in Heel position. After you command "SIT," since you really mean "sit and pay attention to me," you must enforce the "pay attention" part. You might find that simply talking to your dog gets him to look up at you. If this works, praise him as soon as he looks up, and then release him with an "Okay" (OFF switch). Start over. If the dog is still not looking up, you can try gently tapping the top of his head with your left fist. I call this "Knock, knock! Is anybody home?" Often the dog will look up just to see who is doing a tap dance on his head, at which point you praise and release.

Holding food and/or toys works nicely for some dogs to initially get them to look up, but be honest with yourself and understand that if you are holding a toy or food, the dog is looking at the object and not into your eyes. Used for two or three weeks, the food or toy is helpful in teaching the dog to *lift his head,* but not to pay attention. Eventually the dog must learn to look at *you.*

For some really difficult cases you can get very mechanical and physically lift, turn and hold the dog's head so that he is looking up into your eyes. Praise and release.

After three weeks of encouraging the dog to lift his head and watch you, if he doesn't, it is time to incorporate a correction. The correction comes in the form of a game called "You Missed It!" The dog is told to sit while in heel position without any part of his body touching his owner. The lead is snug but not tight and held with both hands at the owner's waist. For some people, I suggest they hold on to their pants so they don't move their hands when performing this exercise. As soon as the dog focuses his attention on something other than his owner, the owner—*without giving a command*—is to leap off with his right foot, to the right, and run quickly 12-16 feet while cheering in a happy tone and saying, "You silly pup, didn't you notice I left? I guess you weren't watching me." The dog is now presented with a problem. He is attached to a leash by a collar, and this leash is held by a crazy person who suddenly "exits stage right" without any warning. It is therefore much to the dog's advantage to keep his eyes on this crazy person.

As you do this two or three times, you can expect that the dog will try to lean on you when he sits. This is because if he is touching you, he will know you are leaving without having to watch you. Do not permit him to lean or even put his foot on yours. You will also notice that the dog will glance at a distraction for a brief second and glance back right away to see if you are still there. This is part of his learning process. Do not leave until the dog *focuses his eyes* on a distraction. Glancing at this point will be accepted. Eventually you will be able to stop him from glancing away with a quick snap up on the lead. If the dog resists the sit, take your time and enforce the sit before you add the distractions.

If you are not impressing the dog in the least by running to the right and he appears to be able to live with being pulled off a sit with a leash and collar, I would suggest you try a more effective type of collar and/or leash. If you are training with a nylon choke collar, try chain. If you are training with a thin leash, try a wide leather leash. If a choke chain isn't effective, go to a prong collar. You must reach a point of leverage where the dog works to avoid the correction. (See Chapter 13 - *Training Equipment*.)

As with all games, there must be a way for the dog to win. If the dog looks up at you for a series of seconds, smile and release! Sometimes when he is giving you total attention, command "HEEL," take one step, and release, as if to say "If you are paying attention, you will hear the verbal command." Gradually demand longer concentration before you release. When the dog will sit and look up attentively at his handler, you have mastered the ON Switch. To maintain eye contact while heeling, start a few steps at a time. At any time that you lose dog attention, DO SOMETHING! Either help the dog lift his head, encourage him, or correct him, depending on why you lost his attention.

Step one of "You Missed It." The lead is held snugly in two hands at the handler's waist. The dog is then tempted with a distraction. *Ron Reagan*

Step two. Without giving any command, as the dog focuses his attention on the distraction, the handler suddenly leaps away with her right foot and runs a few feet to the right while verbally speaking to the dog in an "up" tone. Handler might say something like, "You silly pup, didn't you see me leaving?" *Ron Reagan*

The dog is thrown off balance as he realizes that his handler has left and he didn't see it because he wasn't paying attention. *Ron Reagan*

The dog has learned to win the game of "You Missed It" and in effect learned the value of paying attention. Notice that the dog is not touching the handler in any way. *Ron Reagan*

What if every time you took your dog into the obedience ring he gave you 100% of his undivided attention? How low a score could you possibly receive?

I was asked to help a girl with a Gordon Setter who said she had a lagging problem. While it was true that the dog was five feet behind its owner, the problem, I explained, was not lagging, it was ATTENTION! The dog didn't even know who its owner was, much less heel for her! If you look at the mistakes dogs make in the obedience rings, over 80% of them are due to a lack of attention on the part of the dog, or handler (let's be fair about this).

We know that it is possible to get a dog's attention and to keep it in the ring because we see the dogs trained by top trainers staring adoringly up at their owners, waiting anxiously for their next command. So, what's the secret? How do you get dog attention? Are the stories about bathing in chopped liver really true?

For those of you just beginning to strive for dog attention, I suggest the following: First you must show the dog that it is possible for him to walk at your side or sit in front of you while maintaining eye contact (or contact with some part of your body for small dogs). You can trick him into doing this by baiting him with food or with a favorite toy. If this doesn't work, you can be very mechanical and lift or hold his head with your hands. Praise all desired positions. Once the dog knows that it is possible for him to walk with his head up (two to three weeks), then he must be corrected gently for not doing so. Lead snaps or gentle tugs on whiskers or cheeks often convince him to look up. A combination of your voice, the leash and your left hand giving "love pinches" on his cheeks used randomly is effective. Any single approach used repeatedly is soon tuned out by the dog.

Personally, I never say "Watch Me." By the time you say "Watch Me," the dog has already looked off and you've missed the chance to correct him. I will, however, after a correction say, "Guess what, you weren't watching" or "You missed it."

The biggest mistake made in training classes today is that first the dogs are taught to heel and months later, when a student expresses interest in showing his dog, someone makes the astute observation that he better get his dog's attention! Heeling cannot happen without attention. Therefore, I strongly recommend that you have the dog's attention *before* you attempt to teach him to heel.

Dog attention in the obedience ring is not optional. It is necessary if you are going to earn degrees. The more attention you have, the easier it is to train the dog and the better the dog performs in the ring. You can teach attention with gimmicks, but in the end it must be enforced with correction. If you never take another step without your dog's attention, you will be on your way to becoming a very good trainer.

78

22

Teaching the Dog to Heel

PREREQUISITE: Before a dog can learn to heel, he must know how to walk looking up at his owner constantly. See the chapter on ATTENTION (Chapter 21 - *The ON and OFF Switch*).

HEEL: To walk at the handler's left side, neither forging ahead nor lagging behind; to sit automatically upon stopping. (This is only possible if he is paying attention.)

HEEL POSITION—Have your dog sit at your left side, parallel to you, neither touching your leg nor more than six inches from it. Position him so that the area between his head and shoulders (this usually works out to be his ear!) is even with your left hip. For small dogs, envision an imaginary line from the middle of your hip down to the ground. Keep your dog's ear even with this line. Your dog is now in Heel Position.

HEEL ON LEASH—This is the first heeling exercise the dog will learn. While remaining in Heel Position, the dog will learn how to move along with you, to turn right, to turn left, to turn about, to change pace and to sit when you halt. Be patient! This exercise will require much practice over a long period of time to become perfected, even though it may seem very simple to you.

Introduction to Heeling

Heeling for the ring is the same as dancing with your dog. It is a pre-planned, carefully rehearsed performance indicative of a smooth togetherness between dog and handler—like Fred Astaire and Ginger Rogers.

For a dog and handler to heel well, it appears as though both are doing exactly the same thing at exactly the same time, much like two people social dancing. Logic tells us that this is impossible and that one must be leading and one following. A dog learns to heel by learning to read cues from his handler so that he can tell when a turn or change of pace is about to happen. While each dog watches his handler in a slightly different way and responds to bends, leans and shifts of weight, the easiest way for a handler to standardize his body movements is to be aware of where he puts his feet. Thus, we talk in terms of consistent footwork or *footcues.*

You Learn the Steps

Before you can teach a dog to heel, you must be comfortable with your footwork, like learning the dance steps before you try doing it to the music. When learning the steps, it helps to wear comfortable shoes or sneakers with good side support. This prevents your feet from rocking side to side as you step.

All footcues for large dogs are done with the left foot since the left leg and hip are what the dog sees move.

The RIGHT TURN:

Heeling in this direction —

Notice that the heel of the left foot is almost touching the toe of the right foot. This cues the dog while single tracking the turn. Single tracking keeps your feet out of the dog's lane, so to speak.

Julia Brown

The ABOUT TURN: The About Turn is twice a right turn, so the cue step is the same only sharper.

About Turns are executed so that you come out on the same line you went in on. This is to say that if you followed a painted line, your About Turns would be correct. A keyhole turn is incorrect.

Keyhole Turn

Notice that you come back on the same line. How far you step off with your left foot depends on how fast your dog gets around the turn.

Step one of footwork for the about turn.

Julia Brown

Step two of the about turn. Notice that the feet are heel to heel. This assures that you will come out of the turn on the same line that you walked into it on. Only the right foot has moved since step one. *Julia Brown*

Final step of the about turn. As you walk out of the turn with your left foot, the size of the step you take varies with the speed at which your dog can execute the turn. The faster the dog the bigger the step. *Julia Brown*

LEFT TURN FOR BIG DOGS:

Single tracking

Julia Brown

LEFT TURN FOR SMALL DOGS:

Some small dogs shy away when they see a foot coming towards them. For these dogs, since they are below your waist and have their eyes focused on your legs and not your hip, cue the left turn with your right foot. As the dog sees your right foot come down on an angle, he will learn to back away from it.

Julia Brown

82

All turns must be executed without stopping or pausing. Rhythm should be consistent, even on turns.

Rhythm

For you and your dog to appear smooth and natural in the ring, you must have a rhythm between you.

Start by learning a normal rhythm by heeling in a circle to the left with your dog on a snug leash. The dog should be trotting and you should be moving briskly. You will be able to feel when you and the dog are "in synch," sort of like walking with another person and being "in step." Try to find a popular song with the same rhythm as your normal speed. This will help you remember the rhythm. If songs are not easily recalled, you might purchase a battery-powered metronome which can be easily fitted to your belt.

To do a fast, use the same rhythm as your normal pace but take larger, leaping, running steps. For the slow, count out the same rhythm as the normal but put a pause between each step. For example, 1 *and* 2 *and* 1 *and* 2. This will drop your pace by half. Be careful *not* to shorten your steps on the slow. A slow should be long, slow steps which are easier to accomplish if you lean back slightly as you do a slow. Dogs who start to sit when their handlers go into a slow are doing so because steps have been shortened and the dog is confusing the cue with the cue for a halt.

You and your dog will score higher if you show the judge that your dog really can perform a slow and a fast. Do not try to fake either pace!

To cue the dog for an increase in speed (either slow to normal or normal to fast): Step down on your left foot with a *faster, shorter* step. This alerts the dog to an increased speed while covering any initial lag. When increasing speed, it is also natural to lean forward slightly.

To cue the dog for a decrease in speed (either a fast to a normal or a normal to a slow): Step out with your left foot and do a *longer, slower* step. This alerts the dog that the speed is decreasing while covering any initial forge. It is natural to lean backwards slightly when slowing down.

Teaching the Dog

FORWARD—Begin with the dog sitting in Heel Position. Hold the leash short so that the dog cannot get out of position. When you hear "FORWARD," say your dog's name and give him a brisk, happy command "HEEL." Then step forward on your left foot (that's the one the dog will soon learn to move with). Your first step is a shorter step to allow the dog time to stand up. If the dog does *not* get up and move with you as you begin walking, the short leash automatically keeps him with you. PRAISE immediately and continue walking. DO NOT SNAP the leash! It is not fair to snap (correct) a dog for what he hasn't yet learned.

"Sit" means sit and pay attention! No heeling is started without dog attention.   *Ron Reagan*

HALT—As the term implies, the Halt means to stop walking. In executing the Halt, move *smoothly* to a stop—do not be abrupt. Stop on the right foot, bringing the left foot up into place (dog moves with left foot, remember?). As you step down on your right foot, give your dog the command "SIT," bringing your left foot slowly up into place and pull upward on the leash while pushing down on the dog's rear. Be sure to guide the dog into a straight sit in Heel Position. Every sit is followed by PRAISE.

ABOUT TURN—When you hear "About Turn," you will turn 180° to the right (away from the dog) and end up going on the same line in the opposite direction. (See footwork.) Before executing the turn, tell the dog to "HURRY," then guide the dog around your leg as you do the About Turn. PRAISE immediately and continue walking. Keep your feet under your body and do not trip the dog. Since the dog is held on a snug leash, he will have no choice but to move with your left hip.

RIGHT TURN—Keep the dog on a snug lead. Just before you step down on your left foot to cue the dog, command "HURRY" as you pull him around with your snug leash. No snaps are necessary while you are teaching.

LEFT TURN—Keep the dog on a snug lead, held in position. Just before you step down on your cue step, command "EASY." Hold the dog back in Heel Position. No snaps are necessary in the teaching phase.

CHANGE OF PACE—To teach the dog the cue step for an increase in speed, command "HURRY" as you give the faster, shorter cue step. To teach the dog the cue step for a decrease in speed, command "EASY" as you give a longer, slower, cue step.

Crowding

Dogs crowd their handlers for different reasons. Some dogs pay no attention to their trainers and have developed a system of leaning as a way of knowing where their handlers are without watching.

I once gave a private lesson to a girl who said she only had one problem with her dog and that was crowding. After watching them heel for a few minutes, I stopped her and said, "I have good news for you and I have bad news. The good news is that we can certainly stop the crowding, but the bad news is that when we do, your dog will no longer be able to heel." Needless to say, this was a leaner, not a heeler. To improve this dog's heeling, the handler would have to start over from the beginning and teach the dog to walk while paying attention.

Some dogs only crowd when the handler stops and the dog sits. This is often caused by a handler who pets the dog into his body as praise for a sit.

Insecurity causes crowding. A dog who is not confident around other dogs and people will often hug close to his owner. These dogs should be given lots of socialization and help and should not be corrected for hugging

Teaching the "wrap about turn" to the dog. By draping the leash at the dog's level in front of your legs you can guide the dog around your body as you do the about turn. The dog is held in place and no lead snaps are necessary. *Ron Reagan*

Guiding the dog around on the about turn.
Julia Brown

Teaching the dog to lean into a right turn in preparation for learning to do an about turn. The handler encourages the dog by tempting it to play with the leash. Food or toys are also good incentives to encourage the dog to lean across the handler's body.   *Julia Brown*

close. Sometimes by placing your left hand between the dog's head and your leg, you can gently get the nervous dog off of your leg.

For dogs who are paying attention and are not insecure, crowding may be an honest error or over-compensation. A dog who fears a snap correction will often lean on his owner as if to say, "I'm with you, don't snap me."

To Correct Crowding

ON STRAIGHT HEELING—Heel in a straight line, feet facing straight ahead as you drift left into the dog. This is accomplished by taking a straight step forward on your left foot, then crossing your right foot in front of your left foot, then another step forward with your left foot. Your feet remain facing straight ahead as you side-step with your right foot. The left foot must go straight because if you side-stepped with it, you would be stepping directly into the dog, which would be unfair. After a few days of this, the dog will start to stay away from you.

For crowding on left turns and the inside circle of the Figure Eight, swing your right hand at your side. As the dog crowds, swing your arm across the front of your body and make contact with the side of the dog's face. If you teach the dog to pull his head away from your leg, his body will follow.

For small dogs, do the same but hold a back scratcher used as an "arm extender" to make contact with the dog's cheek. (Few small dogs crowd.)

FOR DOGS WHO HEEL WIDE—Heel in a straight line and while facing forward, drift right. You may also try incorporating a Step Right exercise (see section on Doodling, page 94).

The Forging Dog

A forging dog is a dog whose shoulders are in front of his handler's left hip. Forging is usually a sign of a motivated, happy dog and the best of all heeling problems to have to have to deal with. Nevertheless, a forge will cost the same half point as a lag, and happy or not, the dog must learn proper heel position. If you are bumping your dog repeatedly on left turns, consider he is probably forging.

Since the dog's positive attitude about heeling is important, forging is the last point of heeling we work to perfect. Many handlers like their dogs to forge because it is easier for a handler to see where his dog is when he is in front. Be careful that you are absolutely certain where correct heel position is on your dog. Have an experienced eye observe you, or heel your dog in front of mirrors or reflective windows. Even very good heeling dogs who understand heel position will tend to creep up in heel position as months go by if the trainer is not careful to insist on an exact point.

88

Pointing out heel position to the dog. The head and shoulders of the dog are in line with the handler's left hip.   *Ron Reagan*

When teaching a dog to heel by holding him on a snug leash in position, we hope he learns *where* to heel. Sometimes, however, when the leash is loosened as in preparation for the ring or off-leash heeling, and the dog forges, he must be helped. Begin by enforcing attention to the spot on your hip, leg, shoulder, etc. where the dog should be watching. This is simply done by pointing with a finger. Point while you heel slowly (it is easier for a dog to think while going slowly) on a loose leash. If the dog starts to forge, pull *up* on your leash in line with where the dog should be watching. In other words, we are correcting a lack of attention rather than a forge. The theory being that if the dog's eyes were focused on the point of heel, he would not be forging. AT NO TIME IS A DOG SNAPPED BACK because this causes erratic heeling and does not teach the dog to maintain heel position.

When you first taught heeling, chances are your upper body was turned toward the dog in an effort to see where he was and if he was paying attention. Now, as you straighten up your posture in preparation for the ring, your right shoulder moves forward, causing a forge in the dog who is cued into your shoulder position. This problem is resolved as you concentrate on helping with your body pointing straight ahead while learning to sense where the dog is and if he is paying attention.

Exercises which work to counteract forging are circles to the left, left turns, spirals left, and teaching your dog to heel backwards.

For severe, chronic forgers who usually forge off leash, you can try to perfect the art of blocking your dog. As you see your dog start to inch forward, swing the side of your right foot into the dog's chest and make contact. Then quickly praise and continue walking. Begin this exercise on leash and slowly to get your coordination and so as not to frighten the dog. When your dog is convinced that he might run into a foot, he is likely to stay back in heel position.

The Lagging Dog

Very few experienced trainers have problems with lagging dogs. This is because their dogs are *never permitted to lag.* When dogs are worked on short, snug leashes and never given enough leash to lag, they never learn that they can.

Lagging is a problem of the new trainer who usually takes the dog off leash too soon to "see what will happen." What happens is that the dog learns how to lag.

When your dog can heel on a loose but short leash at all speeds and perform all turns comfortably, why should he ever lag?

Lagging is frequently caused by attempting to train the dog on a loose leash. When the dog lags, he is snapped forward (punished for what he has not yet learned), and he either fears future snaps or develops a bad, lethargic attitude about heeling. Why should a dog be anxious to do something new when he is likely to get corrected before he is taught?

It should be impossible for a dog to lag on leash unless someone allows it to happen! No dog should be asked to heel off leash until he can do it well and easily on leash.

If you have already caused a lagging problem, stop snapping, begging, coaxing and bribing, and start teaching the dog where heel position is with a short lead.

Teaching the Dog to Sit "Straight"

For many people starting out in obedience, teaching a dog to sit straight in heel position seems like a mammoth task. In most early training classes you are told over and over again to have your dog sit straight, only to find that when you attempt your first match show most of your points are lost on crooked sits! It appears to the newcomer that his dog will never learn to sit squarely, and all too often the trainer lowers his standards rather than examining the problem.

All too often novice handlers come to a halt, and when they notice that their dog is sitting at a 45 degree angle to them, they reach down with their left hand and slide the dog's rump into position. Aside from giving the dog hemorrhoids, this does nothing to teach a dog how to line up with your leg and sit squarely. If the dog does not move his own body into position, he never learns how to do it. The dog who has been slid into position learns that he really doesn't have to worry about where he sits because hands will come down from above and fix him.

What is even more ridiculous is the handler who emphasizes "sit straight" as he slides the dog into position. "Straight" is an abstract term which no canine will ever comprehend regardless how often or loudly you command it. "Straight" is also relative. Straight in line with what? Have you ever pointed out to the dog what he is to be straight with?

Another classic training technique is to haul the dog (on a choke chain, mind you) backwards and then to swing him into a straight sit. All this because the dog never noticed that his handler had stopped walking and therefore ended up in a forged, crooked sit. Has the handler here ever considered that perhaps the error is that the dog was not paying attention or that he has never learned the cue that a halt is coming? Does the handler have a way of cueing his dog that he is about to stop? How does swinging a dog back into a straight sit solve an attention or missed cue problem? It doesn't, which is why the dog continues to sit forged and crooked and the handler, in desperation, yells louder, "Sit straight, please sit straight!" (Sometimes "please" is omitted and other words substituted.)

In all honesty, good trainers spend very little time fixing crooked sits. In fact, their dogs rarely sit crooked. The reason for this amazing phenomenon is really very simple.

Pointing out heel position to the small dog.

Julia Brown

If you teach a dog a cue that you are stopping, and if the dog is paying attention and is in heel position when you stop, and if the dog has been taught a point where he should look to line up with your leg, why would he end up crooked? He wouldn't, but so often a sit is not taught, it is just demanded.

To begin with, do not even attempt to teach an automatic sit while heeling until your dog will heel attentively and maintain heel position. To halt when the dog is not paying attention or when he is out of heel position is asking for a crooked sit.

Sit should first be taught in a stationary position. Plant your left foot (in the direction you are facing). Gather your leash in your right hand all the way to the collar. Now, gently, pull up with your right hand as you guide the dog's rump into position in line with your left leg. Slight pressure down on the rump may be required to sit the dog, but most of the force should be in an upward direction which will induce the dog to sit up on his haunches and not slouch over on one hip. Once the dog is responding and will sit on command, point with one finger of your left hand to the spot where the dog should look to line up a straight sit. This spot might be a seam on your pants, a pocket, or your knee if you are training a small dog.

A good cue to your dog that you are stopping is when your left foot moves more slowly, ending up stopped next to your right foot. Handlers who attempt to cue a dog by taking small baby steps are penalized for aiding the dog because it is not considered natural to stop by taking tiny steps. To slow down slightly before you come to a halt is considered a natural movement.

To teach your dog what the slower left foot means, begin with your dog in heel position, "dancing" attentively on your side. Command "SIT" as you step down with your right foot. Then bring your left foot up more slowly to meet your right foot. If your dog has not sat by the time your feet are together, snap (not pull) up directly over the dog's head to remind him to sit. Since the dog has heard the command "SIT" before you actually stopped moving, the snap correction is justified.

For cues to be effective, they must be used consistently. This means that every time you come to a halt, you must stop on your right foot and bring your left foot up more slowly into place next to your right foot.

As a prerequisite for teaching a proper sit, you as the trainer must be able to visualize—from your position next to and above the dog—what a straight sit looks like. Train your eye with the help of an experienced person or a mirror. Finally, if your goal is to train a dog who always sits straight, you must be working with a dog who is physically capable of sitting squarely.

To perfect your dog's ability to line up a straight sit, alternate where the sits appear in the heeling patterns. For example, practice about-turn halt, then left-turn halt, right-turn halt, slow halt, and finally fast halt.

Pivoting in place, one step at a time, will also enforce the concept of the straight sit. When practicing, be aware of the surface you are working on. To try to perfect sits on uneven ground is futile.

It is really quite easy to teach a dog to sit straight, provided you are willing to *teach* the dog how to do it and not merely correct him for what he never learned. Since straight sits are part of polishing obedience, remember to be fair and to be patient.

Doodling

Heeling can be improved by practicing maneuvers other than the heeling you would find in a ring. The following are a group of exercises which you will never be asked to perform in a ring situation. They do, however, offer variety and assist the dog in his understanding of the basic exercises. TRY THEM!

STEP RIGHT—In class the command to the handler is "Step Right." This exercise occurs when the dog is in motion at Heel. The handler will take a lateral step to the right and then continue forward normally. Upon taking the step right, the handler should be prepared to guide the attentive dog towards his leg, or if the dog is not attentive, to give a leash correction and then praise. As the dog is not expecting the move he might be left out of Heel position. If the dog is paying attention but is confused, help him by guiding him with the leash—DO NOT SNAP! This exercise is particularly good for dogs who tend to heel wide but should not be used too often for dogs who crowd their handlers.

SPIRALS—Spirals may be done either to the right or to the left. The handler begins by heeling in a wide circle and continues to walk in a circle with each circle getting smaller and smaller. Eventually the circle should be so small that the dog is actually pivoting. The dog should be helped to avoid either crowding or lagging. The spiral exercise is particularly good for improving the Figure 8 exercise. Dizzy?

ONE STEP, HALT—In class the command to the handler is "One Step, Halt." This exercise begins with the dog sitting at Heel position. The handler is to command the dog to "HEEL" and step off on the left foot. The right foot is then lifted, and when the right foot returns to the floor, the handler quickly commands "SIT." The handler has actually only taken one step forward. This exercise is particularly good for improving the automatic sit of the dog upon realizing the handler has come to a halt.

RIGHT-TURN SQUARE—This exercise is similar to the One Step, Halt except that with each step the handler is pivoting to the right. After four pivots, the handler should be right back where he started from. The Right-Turn Square should begin with the right foot being lifted and turned to the right. The left foot is then lifted and planted next to the right. The command to the dog is "HEEL" and then "SIT." It is up to the dog to realize that the handler is turning, and if he isn't paying attention, a leash correction should be given. If the dog is paying attention and is reluctant, coax him.

LEFT-TURN SQUARE—The Left-Turn Square is the same as the Right-Turn Square except that the handler is moving to the left and the dog must pivot out of the way. To indicate a backward movement, the command "BACK" or "OFF" is used instead of "HEEL." Begin with the right foot, since it is a pivot, and bring your left knee up at the same time as you step with your left leg, which will encourage the dog to get out of the way. A leash jerk up and back will also help encourage the dog to move out of the way.

270 TURN—This exercise is done with the dog in motion at Heel position. The command to the handler is "270 Turn." The handler does an About Turn (to the right, naturally!), immediately followed by a Right Turn. Since the normal Right Turn is 90 degrees and an About Turn is 180 degrees, when combined the handler is actually turning 270 degrees. Most dogs will correct themselves on a tight lead as the handler goes into the last 90 degrees of the turn as they are not expecting it. This exercise is particularly good for getting the dog's attention and for improving the normal About Turn exercise.

LEFT "U"—This is the opposite of an About Turn. When wishing to change direction in the form of a Left U, turn left into the dog and heel back on the same line. The dog must learn to back out of your way. You can help him do this by pulling back on the leash as you swing your right hand and brush his head out of your way. For shorter dogs, use an arm-extender (back scratcher). Left U's are good exercises to use to make left turns easier and to help counteract forging.

FINDING HEEL—Finding Heel is executed the same as the One Step, Halt except that the handler takes one step laterally to the side or backwards. The exercise begins with the dog at heel, sitting with the owner at a halt. While we don't necessarily want to teach the dog to heel backwards, if he can find heel when we back up, we are sure he knows where it is. Teaching the dog to adjust laterally helps prevent wide or crooked sits in normal heeling. Command "HEEL" and guide the dog with your left hand and leash as you bring the dog into heel position. (Doodling maneuvers allow a handler to set up his dog for an exercise without excessive movement or circling. This is a valuable tool in the obedience ring.)

How to Improve Heeling

Mistakes in heeling usually occur for one of the following reasons:

1. Lack of attention on the part of the dog.
2. Lack of knowledge of heeling cues on the part of the dog.

3. Erratic movements on the part of the handler (not smooth).
4. Improper cueing on the part of the handler.

It is easy to say that heeling can be improved with practice, but *WHAT, HOW* and *WHEN* do you practice?

Practice individual segments with repetition and praise. You may choose to work on any of the following segments:

1. Starts.
2. Forward, followed immediately with a halt.
3. Right turn, halt.
4. Left turn, halt.
5. About turn, halt.
6. Right turns.
7. Left turns.
8. About turns.
9. Normal pace.
10. Slow pace.
11. Fast pace.
12. Changing pace (speeding up).
13. Changing pace (slowing down).
14. Circle right.
15. Circle left.
16. Crowding.
17. Forging.
18. About turns with distractions.
19. Quick sits, properly timed.
20. Straight sits (lining up).
21. Off-lead corrections (on specific segments).
22. Walking into gates and walls.
23. Pivots—right, left, about (start on right foot).
24. Play "find heel" games.
25. 270 degree turns to improve about turns.
26. Rhythm.

Work on no more than three segments in one session; vary your emphasis. Make sure *you* can execute the maneuver before trying it with the dog. Never *start* without the dog's attention, and then work to keep it. Work in different locations. New places add excitement for both you and the dog as well as providing new distractions.

Think of heeling as "dancing with your dog" and learn to do it smoothly and in rhythm.

A good heeling dog is a dog with high scores, so get to work!

How long should you heel? Until the dog shows the first signs of wearing out. An older, experienced dog could heel for up to ten minutes; young dogs, a few *good* minutes, then rest.

Heeling with dog attention.

Julia Brown

When teaching a dog to heel, your voice is a valuable tool. Your talking helps keep the dog's attention as well as giving him confidence and helping him to learn the foot cues. At some point in the dog's training, however, he must be weaned off of your constant chatter if he is to heel well in a quiet ring situation. As the dog's understanding of heel progresses, lower your verbal help to a whisper. Then gradually say less and less as he shows you he is confident enough to heel without your continuous approval. Praise will always come at the end of a heeling pattern, but the dog must be weaned off of your talking to him while heeling gradually so as not to destroy his confidence.

23

The Figure 8

THE PURPOSE of the Figure 8 is to enable the dog and owner to walk through crowded corridors, around obstacles and in congested areas that require constant direction and gait changes.

Select two posts approximately six to eight feet apart. These posts may be people or objects such as chairs, trees, garbage cans or whatever suffices. Take a position which places you and your dog all equal distance between the posts, with your dog at the mid-point. Visualize an imaginary straight line running between the posts. Position yourself and your dog, in the Heel position, perpendicular to this line, approximately 12 inches away from the line. Begin heeling, as always, by leading with your left foot. The first steps are the same as for a Forward, Left Turn, and after that you are into the Figure 8 pattern. You and your dog will first circle the left post, walk a diagonal line between the two posts, and circle the right post as you proceed to walk a Figure 8 pattern. It is easier for the dog to go left first because he is going from a sitting position to a slow around the left post.

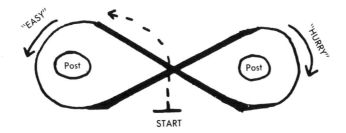

As you and your dog walk this Figure 8 pattern, you will require your dog to maintain the Heel position. In order to maintain the Heel position, your dog will have to decrease his speed as you circle the first post. This places your dog on the inside track between you and the post. Since he is walking the inside track, in this instance, he will not be covering as much distance as you. As you come out of the circle and take up the diagonal track, your dog should increase speed in order to maintain the Heel position. As you begin to circle the right post, your dog will now be on the outside track and you on the inside track. This time your dog will have to increase speed in order to maintain the Heel position since he will be covering the greater distance.

Perfecting the Figure 8 Exercise

The Figure 8 is similar to the Circle Left and Circle Right, and yet the pattern is not really two circles.

The Figure 8, while at first glance appears straight forward, is really a very complex maneuver. The exercise requires the dog to continually change pace from normal to slow to normal and then to fast, and to do all this while walking on a curve!

S = Slow
N = Normal
F = Fast

We begin by first teaching the dog that this exercise requires a change of pace. Start with the dog on a tight lead so he cannot forge or lag. Begin to the left at an extremely slow pace, and explain to the dog with words like "EASY, SLOW" that he is to walk very slowly. As you head into the straight-away, pick up speed, pass normal, and by the time you begin the outside curve you should be jogging with small steps and encouraging the dog verbally with "HURRY, HURRY." Since the dog is on a tight lead, he cannot lag. You might feel like you are dragging him; this is alright. The dog will eventually learn to trot briskly around the outside curve to keep

100

By playing "airplane" the handler learns to shift her weight naturally to single track around the posts. *Ron Reagan*

Practicing double Figure 8s for variety and to work on dog attention. *Ron Reagan*

from being dragged. As you come out of the outside curve, slow your speed back down to normal and then back to slow to go into the left curve. After a few weeks the dog will begin to anticipate the pace changes and you will be ready to go back to maintaining a steady pace as the dog will make the necessary adjustments to stay in Heel position.

WORKING WITH THE DOG—Walking a curve is not as easy as it seems. It is impossible to walk a curve without shifting your weight and leaning slightly. As you walk the curve properly, you will notice that your feet *single track,* which means you will be putting one foot in front of the other. To learn how to properly shift your weight, pretend you are an airplane. Put your arms out as wings. Now imagine that the Figure 8 posts are mountains. Banking as a plane would, fly around the mountains. Glide until it feels natural.

To teach the dog to lean into a turn, hold a toy or tidbit in front of his face as you spiral tighter and tighter to the right. Make a game out of this as the dog learns to dig his feet in and lean into the turn to get his reward.

THINK ABOUT YOUR FEET—Until the dog is very in tune with performing a Figure 8, your feet play a critical role in cueing the dog which way to turn. Cues are made with the left foot for large dogs (as in the left turn), on the right foot for small dogs (as in the left turn). To begin the Figure 8, you start with forward, left turn, to get you into the Figure 8. It would not be fair to say "HEEL" and suddenly step left into the dog to begin the exercise!

There are four critical points in the Figure 8. They are:

They are critical points because at each point you must cue the dog of a change of direction. To accomplish this, you work to reach each critical point on the foot you cue with (which varies with your dog's size).

PROOFING—Once the dog and you are together, smoothly floating around the Figure 8 pattern, to keep the dog thinking, vary the exercise by adding about turns, left U's, circling one post more than another, work with strange posts, more than two posts, and finally work the exercise simultaneously with another dog and handler!

O = Dog
X = Handler

If both handlers and dogs begin to their respective left, there should be *no collisions!* Also vary floor surfaces as the dog needs to learn to dig his feet in and lean more when the floor surface is slick.

24

Teaching a Dog to Heel
OFF LEASH

THE BIGGEST MISTAKE made by beginning trainers is taking the leash off a dog before the dog is ready to work off leash. The second biggest mistake is not knowing what to do when the dog makes a mistake and he's off leash. Good trainers find that the longer they train, the less they choose to remove the leash.

Before you can begin teaching off leash heeling, you must have you and your dog to the point where you can heel together on a short, loose leash, perform all turns and changes of pace, in rhythm, WITH DISTRACTIONS, and the leash is never tight. Then, and only then, should you consider removing the leash. To give you some guidelines for how long this takes: in the hands of an experienced trainer it takes an above-average dog one full year to learn how to heel! I am not talking about the time it takes a dog to prepare for a C.D. title, I am talking about really understanding and being proficient at heeling so that in a ring situation the dog never loses more than one point on heeling.

Every dog knows when he is on leash and when he is off leash. If he didn't, then he'd be too stupid to train in the first place! Many trainers advocate that if a dog makes a mistake off leash, you should put the leash back on and make a correction, then remove the leash. This establishes the leash as a threat. I believe dogs are smart enough to realize that there are times (in the obedience ring) when the leash is not around and is unlikely to be reattached. Rather than making the leash the reason a dog heels, I prefer to use something that is permitted in the ring to enforce the Heel command. The following is the procedure used to teach heeling off leash with "off leash corrections."

1. When you are sure the dog is ready to heel off leash, put him on a light, 6-foot leash and tie the leash to your body. (Tying it to your

belt or pants loops works well.) The leash is there only to prevent the dog from leaving as it is natural for him to attempt to avoid the "off leash correction." At *no* time are you to reach for the leash to correct. It is as if it is not there.

2. Begin with your dog sitting in Heel position, with attention, and start your big circles to the left at normal pace. If the dog makes no mistakes, add distractions. (Don't tell me you can't distract him—try a chicken!)

3. When your dog gets out of Heel position, reach IN SLOW MOTION with your left hand and take a firm grip on the side of his face (cheeks or whiskers work well) and while heeling move him gently but deliberately up *into Heel position* as you let go and, when he is back to Heel position, praise. I cannot impress upon you enough how important it is that you do this SLOWLY. Avoid grabbing and move so that the dog sees what you are doing so he's not frightened. Be sure not to let go until the dog is in, or a little ahead of, Heel position. (A dog who is a little ahead of Heel position will fall into position as soon as you let go and keep moving.)

4. After the dog is back in Heel position, praise profusely, continue a few more steps, and then release him from the exercise.

The first thing that will happen is that when the dog sees your hand reaching for him, he will duck and pull away. Let him! He is tied to you so he really can't get very far. Keep your left hand extended, reaching for him as he moves away from you. Continue walking slowly towards him. Smile! Eventually (sooner if you are indoors) the dog will reach a barrier. When he does, finish your reach, take hold of him and while *saying nothing* walk him back to the point where he made the mistake and correct the error, praise, continue heeling and then release.

After a few weeks of this, the dog will stop avoiding your arm because he will understand that you are not hurting him and that you are simply moving him back into position.

You will know when the dog understands and accepts the correction because as you reach, he will start to correct himself before you can help him. At this point you are ready to untie the leash and you have a way of correcting a dog off leash. Since left hands and arms are still permitted in the obedience rings, you have it made! The dog respects the hand and the hand comes into the ring with you.

Another advantage to having an "off leash correction" is that it allows you to practice off leash heeling. Yes, when you have a way of correcting, it pays to practice off leash heeling.

Heeling off leash is taught step by step, the same as it was on leash. Begin with your big circles to the left, then to the right. Then add the fast and the slow. Next, master about turns, and finally work right and left turns.

To enforce the sit when the leash is off, go back to your verbal sit cue as you step down on your right foot, followed by a swat with your left hand on the rear (instead of a snap up with the leash) if the dog has not sat by the time your left foot comes into place.

When you begin off leash heeling, your dog will make mistakes for different reasons. Think back to Chapter 11 on *Understanding Corrections.* If the dog misses a cue for a turn because he is confused, you should help him by adding the verbal cue of "hurry" or "off" or "easy." If the dog is distracted or is lagging because he feels he has a choice (especially now that the leash is off), he should receive an "off leash correction."

Just because you now know how to correct a dog off leash doesn't mean you can reach for him every time he's out of position. If you reach for the dog when you should be helping him, he will panic and may even freeze while heeling.

While I have witnessed many top trainers use their hands to correct their dogs off leash, I have never heard anyone else attempt to teach it as a method to students. The reason for this is not really that top trainers hide their best secrets, but rather that it is very difficult for a new handler to learn to read his dog well enough and time the correction perfectly enough to be able to use the method effectively. The danger with using the "off leash correction" is that if you do it too quickly, or at the wrong time, you will make the problem much worse. It is also difficult for the beginning handler to watch his dog balking from the hand initially, and few are willing to work to the point where the dog accepts the correction. Students have been successful with this technique, but usually they require close supervision while learning it.

For small dogs, one finger slipped into the collar, VERY SLOWLY, works the same as reaching for a dog's cheek.

If you attempt to learn to correct your dog off leash and find it doesn't work, do not become discouraged. It is almost impossible to learn how to train a dog entirely from a book! Chances are, your attempts are not smooth, your timing is off and your dog senses your insecurity. Like anything else you desire to perfect, much time and effort is required. Whenever possible, seek the help of someone who has already perfected this method.

25

Understanding Difficult Heeling Patterns

THE FOLLOWING are heeling patterns you may be asked to perform in a ring. Certain sequences are more difficult than others. You should be aware of these difficult patterns and practice them from time to time.

In preparation for heeling in a ring situation, be sure to practice heeling your dog into walls, gates and ropes, striving for a straight sit each time. It is natural for a dog to want to avoid walking into a barrier. A "forward, fast, normal, halt" into a wall is a common tie breaker for runoffs.

When watching a heeling pattern in a ring, do not try to memorize it. Make note of the basic pattern, for example an L-shape or a T or an E, and then note any tricky sequences as are described below.

Heeling Patterns and Pointers

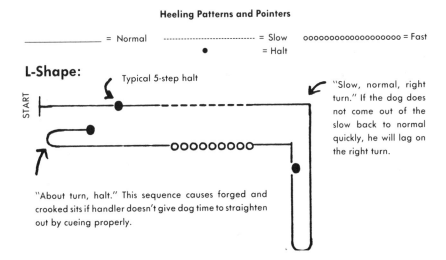

_____ = Normal   -------------------------------- = Slow   oooooooooooooooooooo = Fast

●   = Halt

L-Shape:

Typical 5-step halt

"Slow, normal, right turn." If the dog does not come out of the slow back to normal quickly, he will lag on the right turn.

"About turn, halt." This sequence causes forged and crooked sits if handler doesn't give dog time to straighten out by cueing properly.

START

C-Shape:

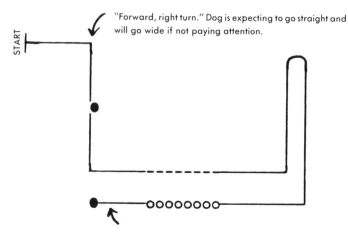

"Forward, right turn." Dog is expecting to go straight and will go wide if not paying attention.

"Fast, normal, halt." If dog doesn't drop back to normal quickly, he will forge on the sit.

T-Shape:

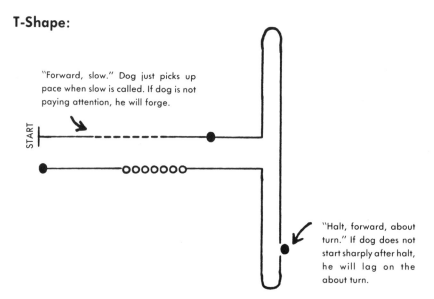

"Forward, slow." Dog just picks up pace when slow is called. If dog is not paying attention, he will forge.

"Halt, forward, about turn." If dog does not start sharply after halt, he will lag on the about turn.

Also practice: "Forward, fast, normal, left turn." If dog does not come out of the fast back to normal quickly, he will bump you on the left turn.

26

Teaching the Dog to Sit

GOAL: to teach the dog to sit on a single command by bringing his hind quarters up to his front quarters, thus avoiding a "rocked back" sit which is undesirable in obedience.

A dog that rocks back into a sit (which is often a breed characteristic, for example, of German Shepherds, Collies, Shelties, Dobes, Old English Sheepdogs and many other breeds) will never score well in obedience since he will either have to forge on heeling before he sits or he will end up sitting lagged.

In Preparation

1. Place the dog on your left side by moving yourself to his right side, if necessary. (This is easier than lifting the dog!)
2. Hold the bulk of the leash in your right hand. With your left hand, palm down and fingertips pointed away from your body, place the leash between your thumb and forefinger and grab hold. Now you are in position to sit your dog.

Teaching the Sit

1. With your right hand, add to the leash you are holding, the snap at the other end. Let go of the leash with your left hand. You are now holding the entire leash and dog in your right hand.
2. Command "SIT" gently, quickly, and only one time. Since it is not a moving exercise, there is no need to use the dog's name.
3. Pull up and forward on the collar as you push gently on the dog's rear with your left hand. Be sure to pull up much more than you push down. Maintain forward pressure on the leash to assure that the dog does not rock back. The left hand is used to guide the rear into the exact place you want him to sit.

Step one: Take hold of the snap at the end of the leash with your right hand. *Ron Reagan*

Step two: Let go of the leash with your left hand. *Ron Reagan*

110

Step three: Pull up and forward on the collar as you gently push the rear of the dog to the floor with your left hand. *Ron Reagan*

Final step: Notice the forward pressure on the collar as the dog is placed into a sit. This teaches the dog to sit by tucking his hind end under himself rather than by rocking back into a sit. The dog is in heel position in line with the left leg. *Ron Reagan*

111

4. When the dog is sitting, release the pressure on the collar and *verbally* praise him.
5. Should the dog at any time get up without being released, *say nothing* and reposition him back into a sit. Praise when he is back in the sitting position.

27

Sit-Stay

GOAL: To *stay* in the Sit position while the handler leaves the Heel position and then returns to Heel position.

1. Tell your dog "SIT" as you guide him into a sitting position at your left leg. (Dog's ear is even with handler's left hip.)
2. Place your left hand, palm flat and facing the dog, in front of the dog's nose (without touching him) as you give the command "STAY." No name is used since it is not a moving exercise.
3. Holding the leash in your right hand, remove the left hand from in front of the dog's nose and step forward on your *right* foot. (The left foot means "Heel," the right foot leaving first means Stay behind.) Turn and stand directly in front of your dog (no more than six inches from his nose).

If Your Dog Should Start to Get Up

1. Jerk gently in an upward and backward motion on the leash. If this does not sit the dog, reach over his back (from in front) and push down on his rear. As training continues, you may jerk the dog more severely if necessary to return him to the Sit position, but initially we are helping him to learn and not correcting him for what we have not taught him.
2. As soon as the dog has regained the sitting position, praise him *verbally* ("good puppy"). Verbal praise is used so as not to encourage him to get up again by your petting him.
3. *DO NOT* repeat the command "SIT." The last command the dog was given was "STAY," which means no moving. If you keep reminding him, why should he bother to remember what he is doing?
4. Keep your eyes on your own dog and correct as soon as he begins to move, but do not dive at him too quickly. Our objective is not to frighten or intimidate him, but rather to *teach* him.

When returning around the dog back to heel position for the first few times, rest your left hand on the dog's head as you walk around him. This reassures him that you have not disappeared and encourages him to remain sitting. *Julia Brown*

Your instructor or a judge will have you execute the sit-stay by giving *you* the command, "Leave your dog." Make sure you give the command "STAY" *before* you move your feet to leave the dog.

After you and your dog have remained in this position for a short period of time, return to Heel position. During the early training, this will mean nothing more than pivoting back to the dog's right side, counting to five in your head, and then praising the dog (verbally). If the dog attempts to get up when you praise him, reposition him into a sit and *say nothing.* Eventually you will return to Heel position by circling your dog. Do not repeat "SIT" and do not repeat "STAY!" The first time you return by circling the dog, rest your left hand gently on your dog's head as you walk behind him. This will counteract his desire to get up so that he can see you.

As You Practice the Sit-Stay at Home

If the dog is not getting up and will sit without moving for one minute, try adding some distractions such as noise, stamping feet, clapping or children walking by. Keep in mind that when your dog gets up and is corrected properly, he has learned something. When he just sits and stays, he is not learning, so we tempt him to get up with distractions. When he is steady with distractions, go a little farther the next time you leave him, until you can go the full extension of a 6-foot training leash. Any time the dog moves, you must go back *to in front of him* before you correct him; when you leave again, do not go as far. Eventually you will be required to move up to 30 feet away from your dog.

28

Down and Down-Stay

THE PURPOSE of this lesson is to teach your dog to assume a prone position on command. The command to be used is "DOWN."

There are two different kinds of down in obedience. In the down-stay, the dog should be lying comfortably, preferably on one hip with one foot tucked. The tucked foot assures us that the dog will not creep. Later on in training your dog will learn a drop. In this down he will be crouched, attentive, and ready to leap up into another position on command.

There are many different ways to teach a dog to down-stay. Puppies are taught differently from adult dogs, and dogs with short legs are taught differently. If you find that as you practice the down you are not getting results, try an alternate method of teaching the dog to Down.

Adult Down

This is for the average-sized dog that is not overly tense or nervous.

Sit your dog in Heel position. Grasp the lead in the right hand at the point where it attaches to the collar. Give your dog the command "DOWN" (in a firm, short, deep tone) and, immediately following, snap down and off to the side with the lead as you push the dog (with your left hand) from the withers in the same direction as you are snapping.

Puppy Down

This is for young puppies or adult dogs that are very frightened.

Sit your dog in Heel position. With your left hand, reach across your dog's shoulders and grasp his left elbow. Grasp your dog's right elbow with your right hand. Give your dog the command "DOWN" and slide the dog's front legs forward (out from under him) gently, using your grasp on his elbows. A downward pressure with your left arm across the dog's shoulders keeps the dog from sitting.

Short-Legged Down

Sit your dog in Heel position and crouch down next to him. Place your

Step one of the Adult Down.   *Ron Reagan*

Step two of the Adult Down.   *Ron Reagan*

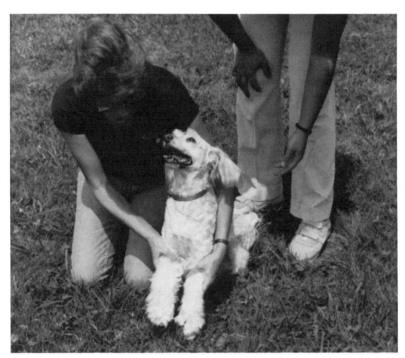

Step one of the Puppy Down. *Julia Brown*

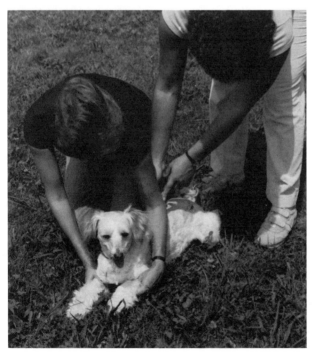

Step two. Gently slide the front feet forward while bringing your left elbow across the dog's back to prevent him from getting up. *Julia Brown*

Step one of the Short-Legged Down.   *Ron Reagan*

Step two of the Short-Legged Down.   *Ron Reagan*

119

right hand, palm up, behind the dog's front legs. Place your left palm on his withers. Command "DOWN" as you move your right hand forward and push down with your left. Be sure to give the dog a second or two after hearing the "DOWN" command before you position him.

Foot Drop

This approach is used for very large dogs, resistant dogs or dogs that may bite. It also works well with handlers who have little strength in their arms.

Sit the dog in Heel position. Holding the leash in your right hand, make a loop (almost like a stirrup). Command "DOWN." Then step into the loop with your left foot as you pull up on the leash with your right hand. Your foot will pull the dog to the floor. If the dog resists, just hold the pressure; he will eventually give in and lie down.

As soon as your dog is on the floor, get down with him and praise him (making sure he doesn't get up). Place your left foot on the leash where it attaches to the collar. This will prevent the dog from getting up as you slowly stand up. If your dog should try to get up, a quick jolt on the withers or another snap on the collar should return him to a prone position. When your dog seems content and relaxed, you may remove your foot from the leash.

When your instructor says "Exercise Finished," you are to tell the dog "OKAY" and encourage him to get up. DO NOT pull, drag or snap him up. He must get up of his own free will. If he is content to lie there, you can always break the down with a "Heel" command.

Down-Stay

This exercise is executed in the same manner as the sit-stay with one exception: the dog will be in the down position, preferably rolled on one hip and comfortable, before you leave him. The commands to stay (hand signal and verbal) are the same and are given to the dog in the same manner. Make sure that the hand signal is given in front of the dog's face. (You will probably have to bend to accomplish this.)

When the dog breaks a down-stay, walk in slowly and push down on his shoulders. You need not sit the dog first. Do not repeat "DOWN" and do not repeat "STAY." That's what the dog forgot to remember! When the dog has been repositioned into a down, PRAISE!!

CAUTION!

• Because "DOWN" is a separate command from "SIT," *never, ever* tell a dog to "sit down" as this is sure to confuse him!

• The "DOWN" command, as with all commands, is only given once,

120

Step one of the Foot Drop.   *Ron Reagan*

Step two of the Foot Drop.   *Ron Reagan*

121

then it is enforced! Do not repeat the command "DOWN" unless you are teaching your dog to count rather than to respond on the first command he hears.

A student who had successfully completed a Novice course once called me with a problem. "Missy is behaving beautifully with one exception," she explained. "She still gets up on the couch, and when I tell her to "Get Down," she lies down and looks at me wagging her tail!" After a long pause I replied, "Missy is a lot smarter than her owner. Try using the command 'OFF' instead of 'DOWN,'" I suggested.

29

Out of Sight, Out of Mind?

THE OUT-OF-SIGHT sit and down exercises found in the Open class should be taught separately. All too often, trainers assume that if their dogs do a sit-stay and a down-stay, they will do an out-of-sight stay. Without taking the time to teach the exercise, one day the handler walks out of sight and that's when trouble starts.

As a preliminary exercise, sit your dog and when you leave him, stand directly behind him. If the dog turns his head to see you, do nothing, but if his shoulders move and cause a foot to move, correct the dog from behind by repositioning him. All too often dogs are left on the stays and as the owner leaves the ring the dog's head swivels around so far to see his owner that he moves out of position. By starting this exercise early in your Novice training, the dog will gain security on stays since he is not facing you but knows you are still there.

To begin the more formal out-of-sight stays, start by leaving your dog and walking all over the room. The dog will eventually stop trying to keep you in sight and will simply relax on the sit. He knows that you are there somewhere but is not totally focused on you like he was in the Novice stays.

Eventually, as you are wandering, drift out of the room for brief moments. As your dog gains confidence, you can be out of sight for longer periods of time.

The final training step is to leave the dog in a formal ring setup and leave the ring in a line of handlers. If you need to make a correction, walk in to the dog slowly and with a smile on your face. Learn to "savor a correction" and avoid rushing in and diving on your dog.

In training and at match shows, make an effort to watch your dog on out-of-sight stays. The object is for you to see him while he cannot see you. All too often, when Open handlers leave the ring in practice, they start to gab and forget to train.

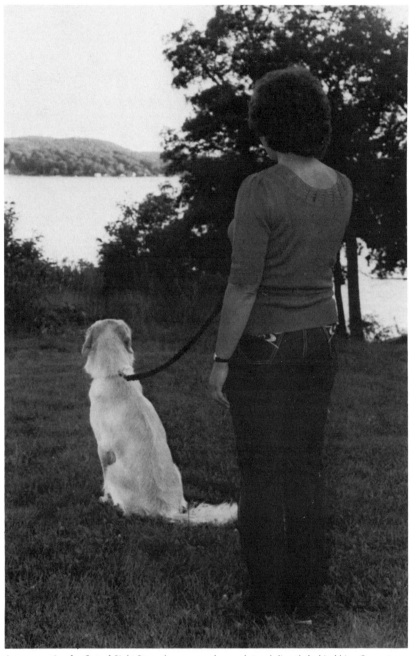

In preparation for Out-of-Sight Stays, leave your dog and stand directly behind him. Correct any movement of feet that might occur if he shifts his head to try to see you. *Julia Brown*

30

Stay Problems

SIT, down, and stand-stay problems can be some of the most difficult training obstacles to overcome. I have observed many severe stay problems caused by handlers who took their dogs to sanctioned matches early in training and the dogs were not corrected for breaking a stay. After a few experiences like this, a dog will be totally confused. He no longer knows what is expected of him.

In teaching the stays, do not rush distance but rather put your efforts into proofing with distractions.

As with all problems, before you will know the best way to correct the problem you must know what is causing it. A dog who breaks a stay to go sniff another dog is different from a dog who forgets what he is doing, which is different from a dog who is insecure about being left alone.

Whining and crying on stays are usually signs of anxiety. Often the dog is staying but thinking about and wanting to get up. Since the dog knows he will be corrected if he gets up, he stays but since he has not yet accepted the discipline as mandatory, he whines with indecision and anxiety. To solve this whining problem, help the dog make a decision—the wrong one. Force the dog to break by having someone nudge him or verbally encourage him to get up. Then correct him. When the dog finally resigns himself to staying, the anxious whining should subside.

Some dogs whine regardless of whether they are on stays or not. If the offender is a male (commonly a Malamute, Husky, Doberman or German Shepherd), it is often a matter of "raging hormonal imbalance," and neutering might resolve his distress.

For females who whine constantly, it may be a hyper, nervous part of the dog's temperament. For these dogs try a stress vitamin program, along with extreme socialization and exercise. Remove any sugar and most fat from the dog's diet which may make dogs "jittery."

Sometimes whining problems can be corrected with the use of a wide rubber band. Place the rubber band around the dog's muzzle. Correct him with a jerk on the leash if he tries to remove it with his paws. Now, with band around muzzle, do a sit-stay on leash. The dog may be quiet at this point simply because he is intimidated by this new training method. If the dog remains quiet, return to him, remove the rubber band and praise.

Repeat the exercise while gaining distance. At any time that the dog utters the slightest sound, return slowly and snap the rubber band against his muzzle. (This is done by pulling it slightly away from his muzzle and then suddenly letting go of it.) After the dog has been snapped with the rubber band, praise for his quiet state.

Once the dog accepts the correction, the presence of the rubber band alone serves as a reminder to the dog to be quiet. The rubber band works to focus the dog's attention directly on the whining or barking problem and can be used on out-of-sight stays as well as for dogs who bark while doing go-outs.

Sometimes stay problems are the result of lazy handlers who fail to correct minor movements because they want the dog to be right! From early training through advanced work, any moving of paws, shifting of hips, swiveling or sloppy sitting should be corrected. If you are clear in communicating your expectations, the dog has an easier time meeting your demands.

If a dog is breaking stays because he is insecure and wants to get to you, there are various approaches you can take. Make a point to hand the dog's leash to responsible strangers from time to time and work to break the dependency the dog has on you. Reteach the Stay exercise with a more gradual transition to out-of-sight as described in Chapter 29. If none of the above works, you may have to correct the dog to the point where the consequences of coming to you are worse than the fear of being away from you. While fear is usually treated with help and a gentle approach, there comes a time when the fear is so great that the dog must be pushed to overcome it, thus the reason for the correction. "Throw chains" tossed at a dog who is coming to you often discourage a second attempt.

When a stay is broken because the dog forgets what he is doing, a mistake in training has been made. The dog has not been taught to do an "active sit-stay" where he is very conscious of what he is doing. Go back to Chapter 27 on teaching the *Sit-Stay*. Reteach the exercise as described without repetition of commands. Remember, if you keep telling the dog what he should be doing, why should *he* bother to remember?

Proofing teaches a dog to think about what he is doing. Have another person command "DOWN" to your dog while he is on a sit-stay. Does the dog respond? Is he aware of what his handler told him to do and what was meant by the command "Stay?" If the dog drops, gently reposition him and praise. You may want to put the dog back on leash and stand in close if his confusion persists. (If your dog responded to every down command he heard at a show, you would have a big problem.)

Another proof technique for a dog who forgets he should be sitting is to put him on a sit-stay on your bed where there is a temptation to relax.

You might even try sitting him and then positioning his front feet stretched out in front of him. While this may be an awkward position, if the dog understands what "STAY" means, he will maintain the position. Correct any and all foot or body movements.

Sometimes stay problems begin because trainers are so busy with the other exercises that they forget to practice the group exercises. This is a common problem for people who train by themselves. Discipline yourself to work on "boring STAYS."

All "stay exercises" need to be proofed. See Chapter 18 on *Proofing* for more ideas.

Stay problems can be very difficult to correct once they start. Take your time teaching the exercise in the beginning and you will have much less to worry about later in training.

31

Come-Fore

THIS EXERCISE aids in teaching the Recall. The object of the exercise is to get the dog to turn toward you immediately upon hearing the word "COME." This is accomplished by making the dog think that if he doesn't respond to the word "COME," the *Boogie-Dog* will bite him! Since most dogs will come when they have nothing better to do, we work come-fores to distractions. Distractions include: food, animals, open house door, open car door, etc.

Steps of the Come-Fore

1. Walk briskly with your dog on a loose lead. An informal "Let's Go" command is used in place of "HEEL." (You do not want your dog looking at you, which would be the case if you used the "HEEL" command.)
2. When your dog is distracted and you choose to do a come-fore, stop, command "Fido, COME," followed by a lead snap if he does not respond instantly (put your "motor" in reverse) and then *back up* (without turning around) for five or six steps as quickly as you can. The lead snap is used to convince the dog that he has been bitten by the *Boogie-Dog*. This snap is done with both hands and is hard enough to upset the dog. Of course, the dog is not upset with you, only with *Boogie-Dog,* who is away from you somewhere. If the dog responds by turning towards you upon hearing "COME," no snap is necessary. Try a more tempting distraction until you can get the dog to make the mistake of not responding.
3. Once the dog is coming toward you, keep the leash loose and encourage him with verbal praise and sympathy (because *Boogie-Dog* got him). Make sure the dog touches you first! Do not reach out for the dog! Once the dog has touched you, you may pet him.
4. Should the dog go past you, turn around and snap him again. *Boogie-Dog* is all over; the only safe place is by you. Do not repeat "COME." Say nothing until he gets to you. Then PRAISE.

IMPORTANT!

- You may only give the command "COME" *one* time. After the command is given, however, you may coax the dog to you with words of encouragement.
- The command to come is: 1) The dog's name, 2) "COME."
- At no time is the dog to hear the words "COME-ON." This is *not* a proper command and will only confuse the dog.
- "COME" means to get to you and stay there. A token visit, followed by taking off again, is unacceptable and is cause for *Boogie-Dog* to strike.

32

"Karate Chop" Recall

THE PURPOSE of this exercise is to teach the dog to respond to the command "COME," no matter what the dog is doing at the time. It is taught and practiced after the come-fore and sit-stay exercises have been mastered. Execute the following steps ON LEAD:

Step 1: Sit your dog. Leave your dog ("STAY" command). Walk to the end of the 6-foot lead, turn and face your dog.

Step 2: Place the loop of the leash over your left thumb and grasp it firmly with the rest of your left hand. Leash should be almost tight, but not pulling on the dog. If the dog gets up, correct the sit-stay.

Step 3: Call your dog with a loud, clear voice: "Rover, CO-OME." Make sure that you do NOT bend at the waist when you call him. The only thing that moves is your mouth!

Step 4: ONE SECOND after you say the word "CO-OME," raise your right hand (fingers together) and bring it swiftly down to your right knee, catching the leash in the middle. This is what we refer to as the Karate Chop. If your dog was up and moving on the command "CO-OME," he will not feel the leash snap, but he will be learning a hand signal to come. If he was slow in getting up, the chop will give an automatic leash snap, and the dog will not know that *you* did it!

Step 5: As soon as your dog is moving towards you, start running *backwards* (so he can see your smile) and cheer him on with your voice. When he gets to you, let him touch you first, and then hug and praise him. It is not necessary to get him to sit front at this stage of training. Coming, although enforced, is always received with exhuberant praise.

CAUTION!!

1. Never call your dog to you and then punish him.
2. Never call your dog to you when he is off leash before he is

Standing ready to call your dog, the leash is looped over the thumb of your left hand.

Ron Reagan

After you command "COME," raise your right hand.　　　*Ron Reagan*

Bring your right hand swiftly down to your right knee, catching the leash in the process.

Ron Reagan

Completing the "chop" brings the dog towards you.　　　*Ron Reagan*

completely trained because if he does not obey, you have no way to enforce the command.
3. Make the "CO-OME" firm but pleasant, loud and clear.
4. Never give the command to "COME" more than once. "Come-on" is the same as "Come!"

33

Teaching Fronts

DEFINITION—A straight sit front requires that the dog be sitting squarely on his haunches, with his weight evenly distributed (no leaning) and his body positioned in the exact center of your body, facing you within reach, without touching you and without putting his paws on or between your feet.

The teaching of fronts is a gradual process. Since it is a precision part of an exercise, it will constantly need fine tuning. Any precision piece of equipment (a watch, a car, etc.) will occasionally get out of alignment. A dog who does good fronts is not a dog who never sits crooked but rather a dog who is easily and quickly realigned.

The only way to get a dog to sit at exactly the same spot in the same way consistently is to teach the dog to focus his eyes on a specific point and then teach him what it feels like to position his body squarely.

Fronts are started in conjunction with come-fores and karate chop recalls. When the dog is responding quickly and confidently to the "COME" command, it is time to add a sit front.

It is important that the sit front be a pleasant experience and that the dog not feel he is being corrected for having come.

To Teach the Sit Front

1. Do a come-fore or karate chop recall. As the dog comes to you, back up. You may back up forever in a circle, so don't let the dog rush you. Take your time backing up as you coil the leash.
2. Coil the leash until you have reached the dog's collar.
3. Your hands, palm down and overlapping, hold the coiled leash, which is under the dog's chin, cradling his head in your hands.
4. Command "SIT" sweetly as you stop moving, bend your knees, lean back and put pressure on the collar towards you and slightly up. It is important that the dog is pulled *towards* you for a sit front and not snapped away from you.

   When the dog sits between your knees looking up at you

Encourage a straight sit front by petting the dog towards you.   *Julia Brown*

Coil the leash until you have reached the dog's collar. Notice how the dog's head is cradled in your hands.
Julia Brown

The handler's knees are bent and she is leaning back from the dog. The dog's head is held to look up towards the handler's face.   *Julia Brown*

(which happens because your dog's head was cradled on your hands and encouraged to look up) on command, it is time to go on.

5. Do a come-fore with the coiling of the leash, but as you back up, change directions. Step laterally left or right just as you finish coiling the leash and stop; command "SIT." Use your legs to gently nudge the dog's rear if he appears to be about to sit crooked. By changing direction just before the dog sits front, you are causing the dog to think about where he is going to sit.

To Transfer Front to Off Leash Recalls

1. Find a point on the midline of your body which is slightly above the dog's eye level as he sits in front of you. For example, this might be between your knees, the space between your legs, a belt buckle, a pendant that you wear, a v-neck sweater, your mouth or your nose, depending on how large a dog you are training.

2. Leave the dog off leash and go six feet away. Point out the spot on your body which, from now on, will be referred to as "front" by pointing to it with your hands or by placing food or a toy there initially to draw the dog's attention.

3. Show the dog front. Then replace your hands to your sides. Call the dog with the "COME" command. As soon as he is up and moving, go back and emphasize front with your hands. Your goal is to get the dog to point to front with his nose. Do not be concerned with his rear at this point. "Front" is a concept, not a command. The command used is always "COME" since that's what the dog will hear in the ring.

4. You may have noticed that a dog has two parts, his front and rear, and that often these appear to be disconnected. To teach the dog what it feels like to line up his front and rear, make a chute out of two broad jump boards. Teach the dog to comfortably walk into the chute and sit.

5. Stand at one end of the chute. Call the dog and help guide him with your arms into the chute and to the focal point of front.

6. To increase the dog's understanding of front, sit him intentionally off center before you call him and teach him to adjust by insisting he always come into you via the chutes.

7. As your dog progresses, you will be able to substitute your legs for the chute. Be careful to guide the dog's rear and not to kick him.

8. For small dogs, 12 inch rulers or large books make good chutes.

Dogs who do nice brisk Recalls and then slow down as they get close to front are worried about sitting in the wrong place and of being punished for what they don't understand. A dog who understands where to look and is

Pointing with two fingers pinpoints "front."

Ron Reagan

Framing "front" with your hands helps some dogs visualize it better. *Ron Reagan*

Guides help the dog place his rear straight while his eyes are focused on the handler's midpoint. *Reagan*

136

Teach the small dog to focus his eyes on the same point of your body each time he comes into a sit front.

Julia Brown

Teach the dog to line up his rear with his front by sitting him between two broad jump boards. The chute is only wide enough for the dog to sit squarely.

Julia Brown

Small rulers work as guides for very small dogs.

Ron Reagan

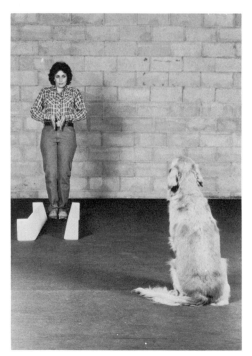

You can teach the dog to think about adjusting to straight in front four feet before he must sit by sitting him off center from yourself and encouraging him to move through the broad jump guides into a straight front position.   *Ron Reagan*

Transfer the use of the boards as guides to your feet guides. Step forward with the foot on the side where the dog is likely to sit crooked.   *Ron Reag*

Always emphasize the midpoint of your body as the spot where you want the dog's attention to be focused.
Ron Reagan

Correct the dog from leaning into the finish by lifting your right knee as he sits.
Ron Reagan

139

helped to line up properly learns to "pop" into a perfect front with no hesitation.

If a dog sits straight but off center, step sideways to exaggerate his mistake as you use your hands to point to front and your legs to guide his rear. *Never step backwards to fix a front!* Most handlers who step backwards end up unintentionally stepping in front of their dog so that the dog never learns to adjust sideways. Stepping backwards would work to bring a dog *closer* to you but not *straighter.* When asking a dog to find front, please stand still!! It is very difficult to line up with something that keeps moving!

Once a dog is used to tucking himself into a straight sit and knows where to focus his eyes, you should not have to work hundreds of fronts to get consistent accuracy in the ring. Be sure to refocus your dog's attention to what you are wearing each day before you enter a ring. This is called "aligning front."

34

Teaching the Drop-On-Recall

KEEP IN MIND that a clear, crisp "DOWN" command, without shouting or threatening, is preferred. Any command is only as effective as it is enforced. Dogs have excellent hearing. "Excessively loud" commands in a ring are penalized.

Step 1: Understanding Two Different DOWNs

There are two different DOWNs in obedience. The first is the down-stay where the dog lies down at your side, preferably on one hip, relaxed and planning to be there for a while. The second is the down-in-motion where the dog drops as he is facing you in a crouched position, attentively waiting to be called up out of the down position.

Step 2: Down in Motion at Your Side

Begin with the dog heeling attentively at your side. Command "DOWN," then drop on your left knee as you slide your left hand down the leash to the collar and push straight down to the floor so that your hand is palm down flat against the floor. If the dog resists and keeps his hind end in the air, maintain your position and wait. When the dog is collapsing before your hand gets to the floor, go on to the next step.

Step 3: Windmill Down

From now on you will no longer drop the dog at your side but will do what we call a "windmill down." While heeling, command "DOWN" and then you pivot in front of the dog to stop his motion, while at the same time swinging your right arm all the way up, around over your head and down onto the dog's neck. (With very large or resistant dogs, you may bring your hand down onto the dog's head or nose.) Your hand is to come down on the dog regardless of whether he drops or not. If the dog beats you to the ground, the hand pets. If the dog does not beat your hand to the ground, the hand will give the dog a jolt to the floor.

Two different kinds of downs. The dog on the left is doing a Prone Drop. The dog on the right is doing a Down Stay.   *Ron Reagan*

Executing the Down in Motion at your side. Notice that the palm of your hand is flat against the floor and that your left elbow is locked in a straight position.
Ron Reagan

This method teaches the dog to drop when he sees the palm of your hand. Never lower your hand in *front* of the dog on the leash as this teaches the dog to drop when he sees the *back* of your hand. When it comes time to drop your dog on a hand signal, if the dog waits to see the back of your hand, it will be too late. The dog should learn to drop as you raise your arm and show him your palm.

Continue with the "windmill down" until the dog is beating your hand to the ground and see how fast you can get him to drop.

If your dog is pulling away from your hand so that he ends up lying sideways, you have unintentionally frightened him. Proceed with the same "windmill" hand signal, but do it in *slow motion* a few times until the dog realizes what is expected of him.

Occasionally use voice only as you pivot in front of the dog. If the dog does not drop, then follow through with your arm.

Step 4: Come-Fore and Drop

Now it's time to integrate the down-in-motion into a come-fore. Do a come-fore and as the dog is coming toward you, command "DOWN" and as you step into the dog, bring your "windmill arm" over your head and onto the dog's neck. At any time that the dog rolls over onto one hip, call the dog and snap him towards you quickly. This works to give you a crouched down because if the dog thinks he is going to have to get up quickly, he is not going to go down and roll over on one hip. Drop the dog at all different points. Sometimes do a come-fore and do not drop the dog. If the dog acts like he wants to drop, keep moving backwards. Say nothing and DO NOT SNAP!

Step 5: Keeping the Dog's Attention

After the drop, sneak away by slowly backing up as you keep your eyes on the dog. If the dog maintains eye contact after you have gotten to the end of the leash, command "COME" and if he gets up with a flying leap, praise him and let him jump on you. If the dog starts to get up slowly, add a sharp snap on the leash after the "COME" command. In the event that the dog looks off (gets distracted) as you are sneaking away, snap him up off the drop immediately as you tease, "Did you miss something? I guess you weren't watching." It is important that you train this exercise so that you have total attention from the dog throughout the exercise. The lead snap off the drop will encourage a fast second part of the drop exercise. Occasionally you should simply release the dog off the drop with an "OKAY!" and let him leap into your arms, which will add speed and enthusiasm to the drop-on-recall exercise.

The Windmill Down: *Left*—Pivot in front of the dog to stop his motion as you bring your right arm over your head and down onto his shoulders. *Right*—Your hand makes contact with the dog whether he drops or not. If he drops willingly, your hand pets him. If he is not in a prone position as your hand is about to reach him, use your hand to give him a jolt to the ground.   *Julia Brown*

After the dog has dropped, sneak away slowly by backing up as you maintain eye contact with the dog. At any time that the dog looks off, give a sharp snap on the leash towards yourself and command "COME."

144

Step 6: Teach Understanding

As you work this exercise, the dog will become more and more likely to anticipate the drop. This is perfectly normal and part of the learning process. We work to cause the dog to anticipate while on leash in a controlled situation before we take him off the leash and work the exercise formally.

Continue working your come-fore exercise, only now as you are running backwards, say meaningless words to the dog before you give the "DOWN" command. For example, "Fido, COME" and as you back up say, "BANANAS," "STRAWBERRIES," "CHOCOLATE" and finally "DOWN." The only word the dog should respond to is "DOWN." If the dog starts to drop on another word, just keep backing up. Do not snap and do not repeat "COME." When you can no longer catch the dog responding to the other words, it is time to go on.

Practice a come-fore drop with a windmill hand signal only. After a few of these, test the dog's understanding by backing up and lifting your shoulders and flinching your arms. If the dog responds to these movements, keep backing up. The dog should only drop on a full, clear, windmill down hand signal. As part of the come-fore, try dropping the dog in exactly the same place ten times. On the eleventh try, don't drop him, and if he anticipates, just keep backing up.

Step 7: Off Leash

Take the dog off leash and do a full distance recall. Since the dog has never done a drop-on-recall off leash, he should expect nothing and come in briskly. If his recall is not brisk, work on the speed before you worry about adding a drop to it, which will undoubtedly slow it down temporarily.

When you have your brisk recall, call your dog and command "DOWN" (in a clear, *sweet* tone) when the dog is approximately six feet in front of you. Immediately following your command to down, begin walking towards the dog with your windmill hand signal. As you meet, bring your hand down to his neck, either to correct or praise, depending on whether or not the dog is in the prone position yet or not. Your walking towards the dog discourages him from continuing towards you. Walk in regardless of how fast he drops in the beginning.

As your dog starts to respond faster and faster to your down command, start giving the command when he is farther and farther away from you but continue walking in to praise the dog. After the drop, release the dog. There is no need at this point for you to work on the second half of the exercise.

Alternate drops with straight recalls. At any time that the dog off leash anticipates and actually drops, say nothing, walk slowly to him and gently

145

bring him to you. Praise him when he gets to you. When he is consistently dropping well and responding quickly, alternate between walking in to praise him and not walking in. At any time that the dog slows down because he is thinking about dropping, say nothing and do nothing. Allow the dog to think about the exercise.

Problems

For dogs who do not stop fast enough in response to a "DOWN" command, you might try the following (listed in order of severity):

1. Stamp your foot immediately after you say "DOWN." (Keep your voice sweet and clear.)
2. Throw a tied up leash on the ground *next to you* immediately after you command "DOWN."
3. Bounce a tennis ball off the floor right in front of the dog right after the "DOWN" command. (Don't worry if he goes to retrieve it, just get him and put him back in position.)
4. Throw a throw-chain or keys on the floor in front of you, or between you and the dog.
5. Tie the dog on a longline to a tree. Measure out where the line ends. Command "DOWN" just as the dog gets to that spot. The line will stop the dog. You may have to go in the first few times and put him down. (Remember not to call him to you after the drop!)
6. For severe cases, hold a water hose in your right hand at your side. Command "DOWN" and then send a stream of water right at the dog.

For frightened and timid dogs, move very slowly and give a slow-motion windmill signal. If your dog turns away from you on the drop, your method of stopping him was too harsh. Back up, slow down and go easier. You probably corrected before you had understanding.

Common Mistakes Made by Handlers

The most common error made by handlers in teaching the drop-on-recall exercise is not letting the dog think. If a dog comes in on a recall and then slows down because he is thinking about the drop, say nothing and let him think! To shout "HURRY" only stops him from thinking and causes him to rely on you to make all the decisions. When the slow moving, thinking dog finally gets to you, praise profusely for the correct decision. The only time you intervene is if the dog actually drops, and then all you do is slowly walk to him and gently bring him to you. Praise only when he gets to you.

Some handlers will not drop the dog if he is coming in slowly. Why not? The dog is coming slowly because he is thinking about the drop and doesn't want to miss the signal. Give him a clear, smooth signal when he's coming slowly to teach him that he will know when he should drop. Speed returns to your drop-on-recall exercise when the dog understands and is not afraid of missing a signal.

Some handlers advocate not dropping your dog except in the ring. You cannot work through a problem of confusion if you don't cause the problem and then work on it.

If we believe that the dog is not wrong for thinking, then he is not wrong for coming in slowly in this instance.

Proofing Ideas

Drop your dog at all different points of the recall.

Drop your dog on all different surfaces, i.e. wet grass, mats, concrete, plastic, wire, etc.

Drop your dog three times in a row in the same place, then do a straight recall. Does he know the difference?

Drop your dog with hand signal only or with voice only.

Call your dog and say, "BANANAS," "STRAWBERRIES," "CHOCOLATE," his name, then "DOWN." Does he know what word to respond to?

Call your dog and make extraneous body movements. Then give a clear signal. Does he know to wait for a definite signal?

Call your dog and have others command "DOWN." Does he know to respond to only your voice?

When you can successfully complete all of these proofing exercises, you are on your way to having a thinking dog who not only performs the exercise but understands it.

Proof the Recall After the Drop

Call your dog and drop him. Now say his name as if you were going to call him. If he moves, put him back. Dogs are penalized for moving on their names; it is called "anticipation."

Make all kinds of nonsensical body motions. Any time your dog gets up from the drop, put him back.

Finally, command "Fido, COME." Make sure that the dog only pops up for the second recall part of the exercise when he hears the word "COME" or sees a clear hand signal.

Practice dropping the dog about six feet in front of you and then call him up off the drop. To encourage him to leap up at you (even though there is very little distance between you), you may need to give him a snap with the lead immediately following "COME" or just release him with an "OKAY," throw your hands up and/or run away from him. For very large breeds, refer to the techniques used to speed up the Recall exercise mentioned in Chapter 17 - *Special Small Dog and Big Dog Techniques.*

35

Left About Turn

THE RESULTS of having learned to perform this exercise will accomplish two things. First, it is another way of changing direction (180 degrees) while heeling, and second it will aid in the teaching of the finish exercise to your dog because it teaches the dog to move around behind the handler on his way to Heel position.

To execute the left about turn:

1. Walk briskly with your dog in Heel position. (That's the easy part!)
2. Pause and pivot 180 degrees to the left (in towards the dog) by shifting your weight to the right leg which will be your lead leg.
3. As you make your pivot to the left, be *sure* your lead is in the *right hand* as you turn inside of the dog, *not* circling in front of your dog. As you start your turn, pass the leash, *behind your back,* from the right hand to the left hand.
4. Encourage your dog verbally as you step forward again on the right foot as you bring your dog up to the Heel position on your left.

The *key* to performing this exercise correctly is in the pivot to the left and the passing of the lead behind your back. Try a few left abouts while standing in place with the dog in Heel position before you attempt the maneuver while walking. Once you are able to coordinate these two movements, everything else will fall gracefully into place.

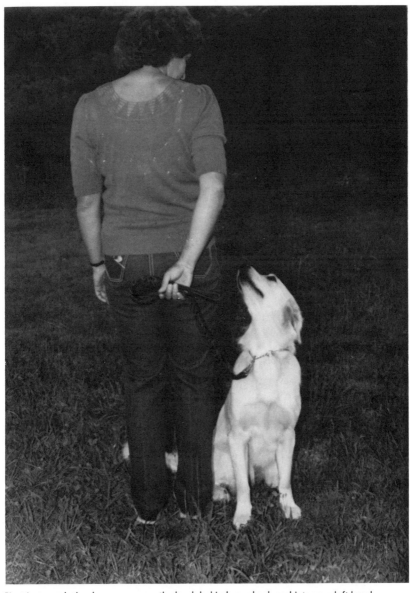

Pivot in towards the dog as you pass the leash behind your back and into your left hand.

Julia Brown

36

The Finish

THE PURPOSE of the finish is to teach your dog to go to Heel position when sitting in front of you. Upon completion of other exercises, your dog will not always be seated at Heel, thus the purpose of the finish is to enable you to have your dog assume the Heel position on command. The finish where the dog goes around behind you and up into Heel position gives you a better chance of a straight sit. The dog has had a lot more practice through heeling in coming up into Heel position as opposed to getting there from your left side, moving towards you.

To Teach Your Dog to Finish

1. Tell your dog "STAY" and step directly in front of him, so his nose is almost touching you.
2. Gather all of the leash in your right hand and position your right hand so that it rests at the back of your right thigh. There should be *very little* slack in the leash.
3. Give your dog the command "HEEL" as you step back with your right foot. If your dog does not respond to the Heel command, give a sharp snap on the lead in the direction that your foot is moving. This will move the dog behind you.
4. Switch the leash behind your back into your left hand, while at the same time stepping your right foot back into place and simultaneously (while looking at the dog) encourage the dog to move up to your left leg and sit. Show the dog with your left hand where to focus his attention to sit straight. Do not snap the dog up into Heel position. Encourage, please!

Large dogs may require two steps backward and two steps forward into position.

Eventually your dog will get up on his own on the command "HEEL" without the need for a snap or step.

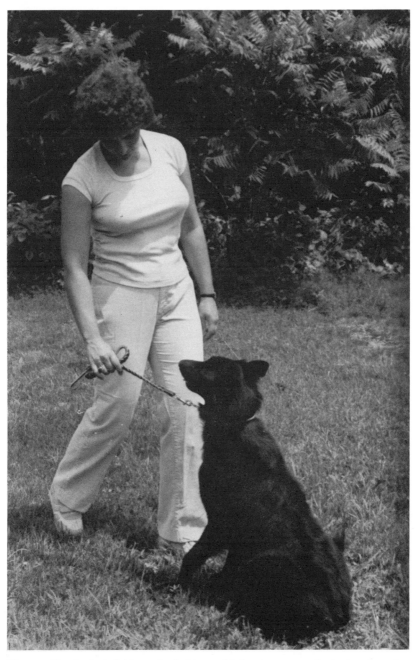

When teaching the dog to finish, step back with your right foot to encourage the dog to get up, after you command "HEEL." *Julia Brown*

By moving the leash with your right hand in the direction you wish the dog to go, you are also teaching him a hand signal, which you will need later in Utility.

It takes a beginning dog weeks to master the finish. This is because you are asking the dog to do a series of things on one command. On the command "HEEL," the dog must get up, walk around you, and then sit in Heel position. In all other beginning training exercises, one command elicited one response. Be patient with young dogs when teaching the finish.

37

Stand for Examination

THIS EXERCISE teaches your dog to stand on command so that you might bathe him, brush him, pose him or otherwise inspect him for whatever reason. It is also a required obedience exercise.

The dog spends most of his time in a standing position during his daily life, and if his weight is evenly distributed, this should be a very comfortable position for him. Most dogs resist the stand position because they don't understand what the handler wants them to do. It seems too simple. Beginning handlers often handle, grope and are in general too physical with their dogs when teaching the stand. Dogs resent being pushed, lifted, prodded, etc. Be gentle!

Teaching the Stand

1. With your dog in the sitting position, at Heel, grasp all of the lead in the right hand.
2. Step forward on your right foot and turn so that you are facing your dog's right side as you simultaneously give him the command "STAND." Place the palm of your left hand at his stifle to encourage him to stand. Lift his head up with your right hand. Make sure your dog is comfortable, with his weight evenly distributed on all four feet. If he does not stand up, pull forward on his collar gently with your right hand.
3. When your dog is standing, remove your left hand from your dog's stifle and place it palm down on his back, pressing down very gently. If your dog should start to sit, place your left hand at his stifle again as you reposition him to stand, and then praise. There is no need to repeat "STAND."
4. When your dog is content to stand still (which may take a week or more), give him the command to "STAY" and step directly in front of him, as you did in teaching him the sit-stay and down-stay. If your dog should start to sit while you are standing in front of him, step forward on the left foot and place your left hand by his stifle.

As soon as your dog is again in the standing position, step back on the left foot so that you are back in front of him, and praise.

5. After you have stood him for approximately 30 seconds, return to the Heel position in the same manner as returning from a sit-stay and down-stay (walk all the way around him). If your dog should attempt to sit as you return to the Heel position, reach down with your left hand and by touching his stifle, get him to stand again.

FOR SMALL DOGS: Those of you training small dogs may find it easier to use a method other than reaching down and touching the dog's stifle every time he attempts to sit. An alternative method is to place the instep of your left foot beneath his abdomen to prevent him from sitting. Or, you may work the dog as mentioned above but do it on a table.

6. After returning to Heel position, praise your dog and the command "HEEL" and heel your dog out briskly. A dog should not be asked to Sit following the Stand exercise as this often adds confusion. The dog might be tempted to sit as you return, thinking that you were planning to ask him to sit next anyway.

For dogs who resist being touched by their handler, or for small dogs in general, loop the end of your leash under the dog's flanks and attach the other end to the collar. Now if the dog tries to sit, lift up on the leash.

Be sure not to let your dog take steps forward after he stands up. Stop movement either by lifting his head with your hand under his chin or by placing your right hand on his chest and not allowing him to walk forward.

For dogs who insist on walking and are too big to restrain, stand them into a wall so they cannot move, or stand them on the top of a staircase so that if they move they go down the stairs!

For dogs who fidget, stand them with their front paws on a platform or step so that their front feet are raised up 6-10 inches.

Touch your dog as gently as possible when teaching the stand exercise. If you handle him harshly, he will learn to stand with his back humped like a camel. Your leash is only helpful to initially encourage the dog to stand up; after that, drop it because you cannot successfully use your leash to correct a stand unless you have previously draped it around the dog as described before. Move calmly, slowly, gently, and deliberately when teaching your dog to stand, and you will achieve the best results.

Before a dog is required to accept being examined by a stranger in the standing position, he should readily accept being touched by a stranger while sitting next to his handler, standing next to his handler, then while sitting in front of his handler, and finally while standing in front of his handler. To assure that the first examinations are positive experiences, instruct the person examining the dog to talk approvingly to the dog and to make the exam pleasurable. For nervous dogs, the examiner might even

154

Teaching the large dog to stand. If, when you touch the dog's stifle he pulls his rear away, bring your left hand under his stomach and up on the opposite side as shown in the picture.

Ron Reagan

Teaching the small dog to stand. Notice that the signal to stand is also introduced.   *Ron Reagan*

Standing a dog with his front feet up on a raised board will often stop him from walking forward or making minor foot movements.   *Julia Brown*

offer the dog a tidbit as a sign of friendship to assure a positive response. If the dog is initially examined with a pat *under* the chin, the dog is less likely to get in the habit of dropping his head as a judge approaches to give an exam.

38

Teaching the Retrieve

What Kind of Dumbbell to Use

While it is true that a dog could pick up any small stick if he wanted to, we try to give him an advantage when picking up a dumbbell. Dumbbells should have tapered ends to maximize vision and should have a mouthpiece measured to fit the dog's muzzle exactly, not allowing the bell to shift sideways. The ends should be high enough to allow the dog room to get his jaw under the bar without scraping his chin on the floor. Dumbbells made to order can be purchased from companies specializing in custom obedience equipment. The names and addresses can be found in obedience publications or through your training class.

Teaching the Retrieve

The compulsive retrieve, also called the forced retrieve, is often a misunderstood method of training a dog to retrieve. A dog who is taught the forced retrieve, in the end, retrieves happily and *reliably*. When executed properly, it is an exercise which is clearly and quickly understood and enjoyed by the dog. If, on the other hand, the forced retrieve is not taught properly, it can be unfair and abusive to the dog. Since many of the Utility exercises require a sound retrieve, it is preferable to teach a reliable, compulsive retrieve right from the beginning.

The forced retrieve is based on the same training principle as housebreaking or learning to sit or down. The dog is first carefully taught the exercise and is then expected to perform on command. Retrieve on command is only as compulsory as sit is.

There are dogs who naturally like to retrieve. The problem with these dogs is that one day, for some reason (usually a distracting situation), they are not feeling very natural! Since so many obedience exercises are based on retrieve, it is essential that trainers have a way to enforce a retrieve.

One of the most effective ways to enforce a retrieve is with a technique called the "ear pinch." If you do not wish to pinch your dog's ear, don't do

A perfect dumbbell fit. *Ron Reagan*

The dog is taught to hold the dumbbell directly behind his canine teeth and not to roll it back to his molars where he might be tempted to chew it. *Ron Reagan*

159

it. For one thing, the correction wouldn't work if your attitude is not positive. When a dog senses that you don't want to correct him, he will resist harder. Usually handlers who avoid teaching a compulsive retrieve get so exasperated at some point in training that they do it as a last resort. It works so easily they wonder why they didn't do it sooner. Do not use any method of training that you do not understand and do not feel comfortable with. Before you get all upset over the "ear pinch," take your thumbnail and forefinger and pinch your *own* earlobe. It is annoying—but not excruciating.

Teaching a Compulsive Retrieve Humanely

Goal 1:

The dog will allow his handler to open his mouth by applying pressure to his lips and place the dumbbell in his mouth just behind the lower canine teeth. (Takes about one week of work practicing six times in a row one to three times daily.) Dog must not fight the dumbbell; he must be willing to let it sit in his mouth before proceeding.

How to Accomplish Goal 1:

The dog is sitting in Heel position to begin. You may stand on his leash so that he cannot leave. Begin with the dumbbell held in your right hand by the ends, hidden behind your back. It is important that the dog not see the dumbbell before he has to take it.

Command "TAKE IT" as you present the dumbbell to the dog. If he does not open his mouth, apply pressure from under his chin with your fingers pinching his lips. Open his mouth from under his chin so as not to block his vision of the dumbbell. As he opens his mouth, place the dumbbell behind his large front canine teeth and close his mouth gently over the dumbbell. Do not allow the dog to throw his head back as this will cause the dumbbell to roll back to his molars where he is likely to chew it. Keep your hands on his mouth so that he *cannot drop the dumbbell.* As he holds the dumbbell, talk softly and calmingly to him and if possible stroke his head soothingly. Then command "GIVE" and take the dumbbell from him. "GIVE" should signal the dog to release pressure, not to spit out the dumbbell.

Goal 2:

Dog will voluntarily open his mouth upon feeling pressure of the dumbbell on his teeth and accept the dumbbell into his mouth. (Takes about three to six days of work.)

How to Accomplish Goal 2:

It is now time to learn how to make a correction in the event that the dog, after having had the dumbbell gently positioned in his mouth

160

approximately 126 times in one week following the "TAKE IT" command, still has no idea that you would like the dumbbell in his mouth. With most dogs, the ear-pinch correction works best because it allows the dog complete freedom of his mouth and breathing. If someone was going to put something in my mouth, I would want to have my mouth and throat free to accept it. For some dogs, however, the ear-pinch correction is not sufficient to convince the dog to open his mouth, and then we are forced to use a collar choke approach.

To execute the ear-pinch properly you must first learn to make an "ear sandwich." Place the extra portion of your choke chain collar (you may need a longer collar for this) over the forefinger of your left hand. Now place the dog's ear with the inside part by the ridges (fairly well inside the ear) over the chain. On top rest your thumbnail. You now have the dog's right ear sandwiched between the chain and your nail, all resting on your forefinger. To pinch, suddenly press down with your nail against the chain. Never pull or twist the ear leather. This is a *pinch,* not a *pull/twist* technique.

There are dogs who will react to an ear-pinch by trying to bite. This is not unusual and certainly not acceptable. If the aggressive response cannot be controlled with a sharp "NO!" then the trainer should resort to the choke collar method initially in teaching this exercise. A dog who is being choked cannot go to bite you. Sometimes dogs snap because they are startled by the ear-pinch, and once they realize how to avoid it, there is no more aggression.

For dogs who are not impressed with the ear-pinch correction, you may reverse the ear so that your nail is applying pressure to the inside of the ear, which is a little more sensitive. Each dog has a spot on his ear where you will get a better response to your correction. Experiment with different parts of the ear to find the spot that gives you the best results.

Why It Works

With the dumbbell in your right hand hidden behind your back and with your left hand holding an ear sandwich, slowly and sweetly command "Fido, TAKE IT" as you present the dog the dumbbell and press the bar of the dumbbell against the dog's teeth. With any luck, he will clench his teeth shut, at which point you pinch, he says "oouch," you slide the dumbbell into his mouth, let go of the ear, and stroke his head as you hold the dumbbell in his mouth. If the dog willingly opens his mouth, let go of the ear and praise. Repeat this a few times hoping the dog will get fed up and hold his mouth shut so that you have an opportunity to pinch him and thus introduce the ear-pinch correction. A dog must learn why his ear is being pinched and understand how to avoid the correction if training is to remain fair and humane. You should never arbitrarily pinch a dog who is not retrieving unless he has been taught the meaning of the correction.

The handler is ready to present the dumbbell and command "TAKE IT." Notice that the dumbbell is hidden behind the handler's back and that the "ear sandwich" is ready to pinch if necessary.

Ron Reagan

Making the "ear sandwich."

Ron Reagan

To accomplish the same thing with a dog who is not impressed with an ear pinch, you might use the collar choke approach. Slide the choke chain collar high behind the dog's ears and hold it snug with your left hand. Command "TAKE IT" as you present the dumbbell and press against the dog's clenched teeth. Suddenly pull up on the collar so the collar is tightening around his throat. He will eventually be forced to open his mouth for air, and when he does, in goes the dumbbell, you release the collar and praise. For the very resistant cases where you must resort to the collar correction, after the dog is opening his mouth for the dumbbell easily you can still go back and use the ear pinch, usually with no resistance. The ear pinch is preferred because while you can choke a dog up by pulling up, eventually the dumbbell is going to be on the floor and it is very awkward to choke a dog down to the floor.

Goal 3:
The dog will *reach* one inch for the dumbbell.

How to Accomplish Goal 3:
Now it is time to teach the dog to *reach* for the dumbbell. It is essential that the trainer be careful never to put the dumbbell into the dog's mouth which is very tempting at this point. We cannot teach the dog to reach if we move the dumbbell towards him. The dog must at all times feel that he controls the ear-pinch correction. His reaching to take hold of the dumbbell gets you off his ear.

Make your ear sandwich and command "TAKE IT" as you present the dumbbell one inch in front of the dog's mouth and slightly above his muzzle where it is easily visible. If, after a moment, your dog makes no effort to reach for the dumbbell, pinch. The dog may try to move away from this spot. Keep the dumbbell in front of the dog's eyes at all times. You may repeat "TAKE IT" slowly in this instance because the dog is often so distracted by the ear pinch that he doesn't remember how to "get you off his ear." (It is only until the dumbbell gets to the floor that moderate repetition of a command is permitted and only then because of the stress you are applying with the correction.) No matter how often you repeat the command "TAKE IT," it is always said in a saccharin sweet voice. You can afford to be verbally sweet because you know the dog will eventually respond. He will make the connection between dumbbell-in-mouth and getting you off his ear.

Distance is now increased slowly. You are always ready with your sandwich for the ear pinch, *if necessary*.

Since the dog knows what is coming, he is likely at this point to try not to let you make the "ear sandwich." If this happens, put your dumbbell away and practice holding his ear. It is not the dog's choice to refuse to let you hold his ear. You own him and his ear!

The dog must now reach for the dumbbell. Notice that the dumbbell is held slightly above the dog's eye level.

Ron Reagan

Use the collar choke approach for dogs who are not responsive to an ear pinch.   *Ron Reagan*

The dog must move towards the dumbbell to put it in his mouth. Notice that the dog is pulling the handler. The handler never pulls the dog to the dumbbell with the ear. This is the ear *pinch* method and not the ear *pull* method!   *Ron Reagan*

At any time in training that the dog reaches for the dumbbell, you cannot pinch. This would be unfair.

Goal 4:
The dog will *reach* six inches for a dumbbell at eye level with surrounding distractions.

To Accomplish Goal 4, apply the same principle as you did for Goal 3.

Goal 5:
The dog will *reach* one foot for dumbbell at eye level, below eye level, and above eye level.

To Accomplish Goal 5, apply the same principle as you did in Goal 3.

Goal 6:
The dog, after reaching for the dumbbell, will hold it in his mouth, without mouthing or chewing it, for one minute while the handler stands in front of him. (Dog is sitting, handler is holding mouth closed. Dog cannot drop dumbbell.)

Goal 7:
The dog will retrieve dumbbell from the floor with the handler's hand on it.

How to Accomplish Goal 7:
One of the stumbling blocks in teaching the retrieve is teaching the dog to pick the dumbbell up off the floor. Here you might have to assist the dog by pushing up on his lower jaw as he has his mouth hovering over the dumbbell. Believe it or not, some dogs don't realize that they have to bite down before they pick up the dumbbell!

As soon as the dog is retrieving off the floor with or without an ear pinch, a quick "COME" should follow after he gets to the dumbbell to insure a quick return. Actually you almost run the two commands together: "TAKE IT, COME!" You can increase the speed of your pickup of the dumbbell by enforcing your "COME" command with a brief lead snap. If the dog comes without the dumbbell, he is pinched until he pulls you back to get it. *You never pull a dog by his ear to a dumbbell!!* The dog must make his own decision to get the dumbbell in an effort to get you off his ear. To date, no dog has ever decided to live with his owner or trainer attached to and pinching his ear.

Some dogs scream when their ears are pinched, others do not. It has no bearing on how hard the pinch whether they scream or not, it's just the individual dog's character. Some trainers feel that the collar choke or collar twist (which accomplishes the same thing) is a more humane method because when used the dogs don't scream. Of course they don't—how could a dog scream or complain when he is choking?

A student once came to me and said, "My dog doesn't like it when I pinch his ear." "Good," I replied, "if he did, it wouldn't work!"

There is really very little difference between an ear-pinch and a collar jerk as corrections—both are annoying and hopefully the dog works to avoid them. Do we find it easier to accept snapping a collar because we've done it longer? Frankly, I'd rather have my ear pinched.

Goal 8:
The dog will retrieve dumbbell from the floor with one of the handler's fingers touching it.

To Accomplish Goal 8, use the same principle as for Goal 7.

Goal 9:
The dog will retrieve dumbbell off the floor when handler points to it.

To Accomplish Goal 9, use the same principle as for Goal 7.

Goal 10:
The dog will hold dumbbell while standing and move with dumbbell in his mouth.

How to Accomplish Goal 10:
If the dog drops the dumbbell, *he* picks it up! Point to the dumbbell and pinch but do not repeat "TAKE IT." He must learn to remember. From the time the dog is retrieving off the floor, the handler never again needs to hold the dog's mouth. Let the dog drop it! Then pinch.

Goal 11:
The dog will retrieve the dumbbell a leash-length off the ground and return and sit front.

To Accomplish Goal 11:
Use the same principle as for Goal 3. If the dog refuses to retrieve, pinch with your left hand as you point to the dumbbell with your right hand.

Goal 12:
The dog will retrieve the dumbbell off of the floor at a leash-length when the dumbbell is placed next to a distraction (e.g. food, another dog or other animal).

To Accomplish Goal 12:
Set up a situation where the dog has a choice of retrieving the

166

The dog jumps up to reach above his head for the dumbbell.
Ron Reagan

Having moved forward and retrieved the dumbbell, the handler commands the dog to come. The dumbbell is held in the dog's mouth as he is led on leash into a sit front. Notice that the handler's foot is guiding the dog into a straight sit front.
Ron Reagan

The dog is assisted in learning to pick the dumbbell up from the floor. The handler pushes up on the dog's lower jaw after the dog has put his mouth on the bar of the dumbbell. *Ron Reagan*

The dog must retrieve the dumbbell from the floor with the handler's finger on it. This is an important transition step. *Ron Reagan*

The dog will finally retrieve off the floor with the handler pointing to the dumbbell. Gradually the pointing finger is removed completely.

Ron Reagan

168

dumbbell or getting distracted. For example, place a cookie six feet from where you toss the dumbbell. If the dog heads for the cookie on your command to "TAKE IT," prevent him from getting the cookie with the use of the leash and then pinch his ear as you *point* to the dumbbell. *NO EXTRA commands are necessary.* If the dog does not know at this point why he is being corrected, we are all in trouble!

Stalemates

It is not at all uncommon for a battle of wills to occur during the training of retrieve. Occasionally a dog will attempt to lie down and die with you pinching his ear rather than get the dumbbell. Calmly wait out his stalemate. You may move the dumbbell closer or get someone else to pinch his other ear. This is called a stereo correction!

Refusing to Give Up the Dumbbell

At any time that the dog refuses to give up the dumbbell, blow sharply in his ear. Really, it works!

The ear-pinch correction is exactly as it states, a *correction.* Just because you now have a way of enforcing a retrieve command does not mean that you pinch the dog's ear every time the dog does not retrieve!

Suppose you toss the dumbbell and it lands next to another dog. You command your dog to "TAKE IT" and he trots out briskly towards the dumbbell. As he approaches the dumbbell, you see that he slows down and his eyes focus on the dog laying next to his dumbbell. Your dog slinks back to you without the dumbbell. Do you correct the dog with an ear-pinch? Absolutely not. The dog refused to retrieve because he was afraid. Fear is not initially treated with a correction. The good trainer (who had read the chapter in this book on understanding corrections) would help the dog by going with the dog to assure him that it was in fact safe to retrieve the dumbbell next to the dog. Of course, the trainer needs to be sure that it is in fact safe to do so!

Suppose after three or four times of showing the dog that he can safely retrieve the dumbbell the dog still refuses to retrieve. Do you pinch his ear? Yes, at this point the dog is making a decision based on his belief that he has a choice as to whether or not to retrieve alone, and dogs who feel they have a choice *are corrected.* Of course, you might also look at it as the dog is still afraid to retrieve the dumbbell alone. This may be true, but now we conclude that the dog's decision is not to make an effort to overcome his fear. The correction will convince the dog that it pays to be brave.

Another instance when you would not correct with an ear-pinch would be if the dog was confused. Suppose you borrowed a friend's dumbbell and the first time you sent the dog to retrieve it he went out, smelled that it was not his, and came back without it. This is a time to help the dog, perhaps by going out with him to encourage him or by actually putting the dumbbell in his mouth.

The ear-pinch is a valuable training aid when taught properly and applied with understanding. The same is true of most corrections. Be careful that you know why a dog is not responding before you hastily correct. A dog who exhibits fear or confusion does not deserve a correction!

Learning, in general, is stressful; and for some dogs, retrieving is *very* stressful. As long as you are sure that you are being fair to your dog, do not fall victim to feeling guilty about having to correct. Try to ignore temper tantrums and screams as you remind yourself that you have taught the retrieve slowly, step-by-step, and fairly and that the dog is very well aware that all he has to do to get you off his ear is to put the dumbbell in his mouth. For many people, dominance, true ownership and control over a dog are not accomplished until after the dog has agreed to retrieve on command. Following the teaching of the retrieve, there is often a new bond, a respectful, adoring relationship that begins to grow between dog and trainer.

39

The Teaching of Scent Discrimination

PREMISE: This method of teaching scent discrimination presumes that the dog has been taught a compulsive retrieve in Open work.

Equipment:

1. Unless you have a very small dog, the single bar type of scent article is preferable since if you have done your work in Open, you should have no mouthing problems with the scent articles.
2. You will need to purchase a wooden peg board, or rubber mat or piece of carpet large enough so that the dog will be unable to retrieve the entire mat or board. Usually 3 feet by 3 feet is sufficient. Tie a handle to the board or mat so that you can move it without touching it.
3. Purchase a roll of wire (the same color as the metal articles). Electric fence wire works nicely.
4. And finally, you will need a pair of kitchen tongs and a pair of rubber gloves.

Before You Begin:

1. Understand that the dog already knows how to scent. You are only really teaching him to do it on command.
2. Since you do not have this terrific scenting ability, you must be very careful *not* to overly correct the dog for bringing you the wrong article because you can't smell what he might have smelled. You will learn how to deal with this error properly later on.
3. Since you are teaching scent *discrimination,* be very careful not to get scent all over the articles, which are supposed to be free from your scent, or to contaminate the board or mat on which you are working. Avoid having your leash drag through the articles. Give

The Scent Article Peg Board is prepared with four metal articles tied down. Notice that the handle on the board allows it to be carried without being contaminated with the handler's scent.

Ron Reagan

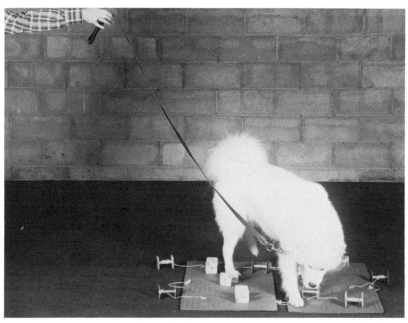

The handler is careful to hold the leash high above the dog's head so that it does not drag through the articles and put scent on them.

Ron Reagan

common sense a chance and do not store your board in your clothes closet!

4. Never put the tongs or your Utility gloves *into* the scent article case as this will contaminate the articles with your scent.

5. Avoid using "Off" spray on you or the dog, as well as perfume or perfumed soaps, when you are planning to work scent. In fact, don't even wash your hands immediately before you plan to work scent.

6. When teaching scent work, do not push for speed; work for understanding and confidence on the part of the dog. As the dog gains confidence and succeeds, he will gain speed.

7. Avoid meals heavily seasoned with garlic if you are planning to work scent; the garlic odor may come through the pores of the skin, and some dogs resent this odor.

8. If you or your dog are taking any medication (particularly antibiotics), do not be surprised if your dog becomes confused when working articles. A pharmacist can usually tell you if "odor" is a property of the drug you are taking. If it is, there is a chance it will change your scent, which may confuse your dog.

Mistakes Commonly Made by Handlers:

1. A common mistake is emphatically telling the dog "NO" when he brings you the wrong article; consequently, the dog decides to stop trying altogether. For all you know, the article the dog brought might have had some scent left over from a week or two ago when it was last used, and the dog doesn't understand why this is all of a sudden wrong. He often becomes confused and stops trying.

2. Handlers get sloppy about airing their articles and cases and about washing and airing the articles they are using. I like to rinse used articles in cold water and then air them for 24 hours or more.

3. A handler should not praise the dog as he indicates a correct article or before the dog has made the decision to return with the article. This causes the dog to put his mouth over an article and wait for the praise before he is sure it's the right one. Verbal praise should come only after the dog has made the decision to bring a particular article back.

4. Some handlers get upset when the dog paws the article to see which one is free. While it is true that he is not using his nose yet, all dogs figure it out in time. This is a normal learning process. The dog will always choose the easiest path to accomplish a task and will eventually figure out that it's easier just to smell for the right article. Working in a dark room will sometimes encourage the dog to start using his nose.

5. Handlers sometimes forget to place the articles at least six inches apart from one another. Scent travels, and this can be confusing to a dog who is first learning the exercise, especially for Collies and other long-nosed breeds whose mouth, nose and eyes are relatively far apart from each other.
6. Handlers make the mistake of taking the dog off leash too soon, and then they take the articles off the board before the dog is truly confident or has been proofed.
7. Handlers have even been known to forget which article they scented!!!

The Step-by-Step Process:

1. Get the dog to retrieve, off the floor, the leather and metal articles (the ones with no numbers on them or the "0" or "6") willingly and with distractions. Treat it as if you were working a flat retrieve of the dumbbell exercise. Make sure the dog is not mouthing and that the pickup of both the metal and leather articles is quick and clean.
2. *PREPARE THE BOARD:* If *you* prepare the board, wear the rubber gloves; otherwise enlist the help of someone else. Tie down two metal articles (with numbers) onto the board or mat loosely (in two places) with the metal wire. For small dogs, you may tie down articles with rubber bands. The articles should have some mobility, but they should be unable to be pulled off the board. The tied articles should be very far apart from one another and in different directions. Now you are ready to begin.
3. *ON LEASH:* Position the dog, on leash, approximately six feet from the board in Heel position, facing the article board. Scent your blank metal article by *holding* it (do not rub it vigorously) for one minute. Leave the dog with a stay command and walk out and place it on the board, making sure it is at least six inches from the other two tied articles (the dog is watching you do this). Return to the dog. Make a cup out of your right hand and place it three inches in front of the dog's nose. (He will have no idea what you are doing, but this will later become a legal cue to him that you are about to work scent.) Command "TAKE IT" or whatever command you have been using for the dumbbell retrieve. Motion forward with your right hand, holding the leash high in the air so that it does not drag through the articles. By motioning forward with the leash you are saying to the dog, "Go ahead of me, it's alright." Once the dog finds the free article *and starts back with it,* PRAISE. Avoid the habit of taking a step backwards as the dog picks up the correct article, for this too becomes an extra cue.

If the dog attempts to pick up a tied article, say nothing. If he gets distracted or gives up and isn't looking for the free article, treat it as you would a retrieve correction and pinch his ear as you point to the scented article. Repeat this step until the dog has retrieved three times without the need of a retrieve correction. If you are working with a very insecure, sensitive dog who is exhibiting confusion, *help* the dog by pointing out the scented article rather than correcting a non-retrieve. This is where "reading your dog" is critical. Why is the dog not attempting to retrieve? Is he confused? Afraid? Distracted? Or does he feel he has a choice? The answer to this question will determine whether you pinch or just point. We can readily assume that if a dog is smelling the mat or grass *between* the articles, he is distracted and is not working the exercise.

4. Now repeat Step 3 but change your command to "FIND IT." Most dogs barely notice you changed the command. From now on you will use the "FIND IT" command.

5. Turn the dog so that his back is toward the board. Repeat Step 3. (Hope he cheats and turns his head to see what you are doing.) Give your cup cue to him, replace your right hand to your side, and then turn after you have given the command. If the dog comes to a sit at your side, gently pull him toward the board with the leash and, if necessary, take a step toward the board. After each retrieve, rotate the board so as to present the dog with a different picture. Repeat this until the dog has made at least one attempt to pull on a tied article. When the dog is readily leaving your side and finding the correct article (he is probably not scenting yet, just trying or guessing), go on to the next step.

6. Have a friend—or use your gloves—add two more metal articles randomly (but six inches apart) to the board. Continue as in Step 5. This is usually the point at which the dog discovers his nose. Each dog figures it out at a different rate—some in a day or two, some in a week or two. Do not become discouraged and do not try to help the dog. If the dog is still cheating (looking to see where you put the article) at this point, then place him around a corner so he can't cheat. (Of course, if he cheats later on in the ring, there is nothing the judge can do about it.) When you are fairly sure the dog is using his nose, get another person to act as a steward and put the article out for you. Make sure the steward does not touch the article with your scent on it.

7. Have the steward (your assistant or friend) touch each of the tied-down metal articles. Now you are asking the dog to find your scent when there is other scent out there instead of just discriminat-

ing between scent and no scent. (Dog is still ON LEASH.) When the dog has been successful and you have used approximately 10 different people to scent the tied-down articles, go on.

8. Take the leash off. The dog still cannot make a mistake because the wrong articles are still tied down. The only thing he might do is get distracted and stop working; this results in a retrieve correction with you pointing to the correct article. Continue to turn the board and change stewards. Intentionally set up distractions around the board, i.e. people barking, noise, stamping feet, alarm clock, other dogs, cat, food, etc. When the dog has made no attempt to refuse to try for one week, go on.

9. Repeat Step 8 but add distance (15 feet) between you and the board. By adding distance, you will know if the dog is truly confident. Dog is still off leash. Continue adding distractions to mess up the dog; keep correcting, or helping if the dog shows fear or confusion.

10. Take all the metal articles off the board and put the dog back on leash. Start over back at Step 3 using only leather articles. Usually the leather goes faster because the dog already has an idea what you want. When you reach Step 9 with the leather articles, go on. Be aware that leather has a strong scent of its own which may cause initial confusion.

11. Using your gloves, tie three metal and three leather articles (with numbers) down on the board. Use the blank scented leather and metal articles alternately. Start back at Step 4. When the dog will do both leather and metal off leash confidently at 15 feet, with the use of the steward and the steward's scent, it is time to go on. Add distractions.

12. Retie one of the metal articles on the board using a 6-inch string (using gloves). The strings allow you to place the articles off the tie-down board without chancing that the dog could make a mistake. Strings also help dogs distinguish between articles that bear your scent being correct versus retrieving the article that moves and that the dog might think is loose. If the dog does not make a mistake in three days, do the same for one leather article. These articles are still tied down, but they are on 6-inch strings. If the dog is doing well with the one metal and one leather article loosened on the board, go on.

13. Start placing your 6-inch tied unscented metal and/or leather article off the board and the scented one sometimes off and sometimes on the board. If the dog is still getting it right, go on. Add distractions.

14. Retie one more metal and one more leather article on 6-inch strings and continue with Step 13. *Gradually* you will get them all

tied on string and more of them off the board than on the board. They are still tied down, but on loose strings! Add distractions! *See if you can get the dog to panic and grab a wrong article.* When you can no longer get the dog to make a mistake, go on to Step 15.

15. Take the board away but save it because you never know when you might need it to straighten out confusion that you might have caused by going through the steps too quickly. You can always back up and start over to correct confusion. Make sure you always use tongs to put out the articles that you don't want to have your scent on.

Once the board is removed, begin with two leather and two metal articles in the pile. As the dog exhibits confidence, add articles. As part of proofing, you might want to build up to a pile of 20 or more articles. By increasing the number of articles the dog must search through, you are teaching the dog to be patient and to work the pile until he finds it. A dog who is used to working 20 articles in a pile is very confident when sorting through nine in a ring situation!

If at any time the dog brings you the wrong article, let him come in to you but as he is about to sit, point back to the pile and command "FIND IT" again in the same sweet tone in which you originally gave the command. Praise only for the correct article. Initially you may have to go out and point to the correct article while the dog still has the wrong one in his mouth. Gently help the dog to drop the wrong one and pick up the right one. Eventually your pointing finger will cue the dog to go back and recheck the pile because something is wrong.

Remove any incorrect article the dog has touched until it has been washed and aired. Beginning dogs will frequently bring an article that has their scent on it as easily as if it had your scent. The only time you correct the dog with an ear-pinch is when he refuses to retrieve because he is distracted or feels he has a choice.

Take your blank articles that you started with, wash them, air them, and put them on a shelf somewhere for about a month. They have become so impregnated with your scent from being used over and over again that they can often start confusion. Air all new sets of articles and article cases before using them.

Proofing Articles

Once the dog is doing articles all off the board and is rarely making a mistake, it is again time to proof him. Proofing adds interest and builds dog and handler confidence.

177

1. Do articles on all different kinds of surfaces (concrete, freshly cut grass, tall grass, tile, carpet, blacktop, etc.).
2. Stand all articles on end, including the scented ones.
3. Use two sets of articles at once. This will teach the dog patience because he will have to check through more articles to find the right one.
4. Do articles in all kinds of weather—rain, heat, cold, snow, wind.
5. Place the articles in different configurations on the floor (a square, an "X", an oblong).
6. Place articles closer than six inches apart for the experienced dog to teach him to discriminate carefully.
7. Have two or more dogs work a pile of articles simultaneously!
8. Put balls and bones and even cookies out among the articles. These are distractions. Make sure they do not have your scent on them. Allow the dog to sniff them briefly, but if he attempts to pick one up and play with it, treat it as a correction for a retrieve. If he retrieves it, treat it as a wrong article and send him back without a correction.

SPECIAL NOTE: If the dog brings you the right article, praise him and do the next article. *Do not repeat* a correct performance. Throughout training, if the dog made a mistake, he had to try again to correct his actions. If you repeat a *correct performance,* you run the risk of confusing the dog. He might think it was wrong, which is why he is being asked to repeat it.

Observing Dogs Learning Articles

Most dogs eventually develop a system of working a pile of articles. For example, they might always start on the left side and work counter-clockwise and toward the center. A dog first learning to do articles may become overwhelmed by a scatter of articles and might tend to repeatedly miss checking one corner of the pile. To teach a dog to work articles, systematically, start by placing them in a line. Once the dog learns to move from one to another down the line, try a semi-circle. Eventually place the articles in a complete circle. As a final step, place one and then eventually more articles in the middle of the circle.

Dogs first learning to do scent discrimination are often found placing their mouths over each article. This is referred to as "open-mouth scenting" and disappears as the dog becomes confident with the exercise. Some dogs even go as far as to lick the articles as if they were trying to taste the scent. In the early teaching phases, ignore this behavior. Most dogs eventually take the easiest route, which is to briefly sniff each article.

Licking articles is sometimes seen in an experienced dog when the

The dog is proofed with turtles once he is doing articles off the board.   *Ron Reagan*

Proofing with two dogs and turtles. Notice that the proofing is started while the articles are still on the tie down peg boards.   *Bauman*

179

handler is very nervous, has sweaty palms, and over-scents the article. In this situation, the dog may indicate the correct article, lick it and then continue to check other articles. This sequence is repeated until some time has passed, allowing the scented article to "cool down," at which point the dog readily retrieves it. It is virtually impossible to scent an article the same amount each time, especially if the handler is the nervous type. Therefore, from the standpoint of training, even though we may understand why the dog is avoiding the correct article, he should be corrected to retrieve the over-scented article. It is not up to the dog to decide when to pick up the article. He must learn to pick it up as soon as he indicates it is the correctly scented article. It is true that a dog may initially be confused by the smell of a sweaty, over-scented article. If you believe this to be the case, then help the dog by encouraging him to pick it up right away the first few times. If, however, the licking and avoidance pattern continues, a correction is justified.

New Utility dogs, often insecure about doing articles, frequently pick up the correct article, start back with it and then doubt their choice and either go back and recheck the pile with the article in their mouth or, more often, drop the correct article, recheck the pile and then pick up the dropped, correct article and come in with it. If this occurs in the first few months during which the dog is working off the tie-down board, the best thing a handler can do is to say nothing, not aid the dog, and let the dog work it through. In some rare cases of very insecure dogs, this behavior continues for months and then needs to be stopped. The dog is usually always right, he just doesn't trust himself. For this type of dog you need to incorporate the rule that: "The one you first touch is the one you take." To accomplish this, correct the dog at the point at which he either drops the correct article or heads back to recheck. A correction at this point in training usually gives the dog the added confidence he is lacking to help him trust his decision.

Some Utility dogs approach a pile of articles, circle the pile, nose high above the articles, two to six times before getting down to the business of discrimination. Handlers who allow this argue that the dogs are air-scenting. While it is believed that scent rises off of an object in a spiraling fashion, I believe this circling of the pile is an unnecessary, bad habit, accidentally learned by the dog. This same dog could just as easily have been taught to go out to the pile with the intent of sniffing each article directly (and not the space between the articles, either). Any time a dog approaches a pile of articles and his nose does not drop in the direction of the articles, assume he is distracted and correct him! You would be surprised how many dogs take advantage of the time they are given to work the scent articles. Don't be fooled!

While it is impossible to determine how long an individual dog will take to master scent discrimination, following the procedures outlined in this chapter should take between five and 12 months. Most of the training effort will go into proofing and building confidence in the dog. Dogs catch on to the task of scent work in a matter of weeks, but it takes months of proofing and practice for them to gain proficiency and the confidence to do scent work anywhere and any time you say.

A dog's sense of smell is much greater than most Utility handlers are willing to admit. It has been demonstrated that dogs can track 6-hour old tracks and smell gas leaks under miles of frozen ground. Knowing this, how difficult can scent articles be? Most errors in scent work are due to insecure dogs (whose handlers have helped them too much in practice) and to dogs who get distracted as they *pretend* to be working.

40

Directed Retrieve

FOR THIS EXERCISE you will need three predominantly white work gloves and a 20-foot long line.

Before you begin: If you are training a small dog, buy boys' work gloves, then wash them in very hot water and put them in a hot dryer in an attempt to shrink them as small as possible.

Stuff your gloves with rags or paper to give them substance. This will encourage your dog to open his mouth when he goes to pick up the glove instead of holding the tip of a finger of the glove in his teeth. Dogs who do not go out to retrieve with the intention of opening their mouths and stuffing the entire glove into it often drop gloves.

Step One: Retrieve of the Glove

Tell your dog to stay, toss the glove and have your dog retrieve it as if it were a dumbbell. Use the "TAKE IT" retrieve command. Correct any mouthing or shaking of the glove. If the dog refuses the glove once he has been introduced to it, make a retrieve correction. Note: no signal has been used yet.

Step Two: Learn How to Give the Signal

The AKC Regulations state: *The handler will give his dog direction to the designated glove with a single motion of his left hand and arm along the right side of the dog, and will give the command to retrieve either simultaneously with or immediately following the giving of direction.* I prefer to give the command "TAKE IT" *immediately following* the direction for it gives the dog more time to focus his attention on the direction.

To give a clear signal, keep your fingers together and your thumb down (otherwise it may block his vision). Begin the signal from behind the dog's right ear and bring it forward in a *straight line,* slowly, and so that the top of your hand is at the bottom of his eyes.

A proper glove signal. Notice that the fingers are together, the thumb is down and the top of the hand is in line with the bottom of the dog's eye. *Julia Brown*

Be careful that your signal is pointing directly to the glove, which means your hand will be tilted down towards the floor.

As soon as your hand stops moving (although it may move slowly), you must then command, "TAKE IT" without jerking your arm or hand. As the dog leaves for the glove and is past your hand, you may return your arm to your side and stand up.

Step Three: Teach the Dog That the Signal Means to Look for the Glove

Begin with one stuffed glove, held in your right hand, hidden behind your back from the dog.

With your dog sitting in Heel position, give him a signal to do nothing. As your left arm is extending, toss the glove with your right hand to where your signal is pointing. The tossed glove should get your dog's attention. As soon as he notices the glove, send him to retrieve it immediately. You may give a signal in all different directions as long as you toss the glove in the direction you are pointing.

Do this until, when you start to give a signal, the dog looks out straight ahead in anticipation of a glove.

Step Four: Teach the Dog That There Is More Than One Glove and the Difference Between Retrieve and Directed Retrieve

Start with the dog sitting in Heel position and with two stuffed gloves. With the dog watching, throw one glove to your left and then one glove to your right. You and the dog are now facing no glove in the middle.

Give the dog a signal to the left glove. If he looks, praise him but don't send him. Then give him the signal to the right glove. If he looks, praise him and then send him to retrieve it. (Dog is on a leash long enough to reach the gloves.) Take the glove and again face the middle. Throw the glove the dog just retrieved back to the right. (This will get the dog's attention.) Now give him a signal to the left. If he looks, praise him and then send him for the glove.

If he is still focused on the other glove, wait a few seconds with your signal pointed to the left glove. If his attention is not drawn back to the left glove, command "TAKE IT" anyway and walk with your signal all the way to the glove. The dog is on leash for control. This exercise is teaching the dog to retrieve what you point to and not what he sees thrown. It distinguishes retrieve from *directed* retrieve.

Continue alternating between sending the dog for the glove you threw and the one you didn't. Do not get into a pattern—be unpredictable.

Gradually add distance to the two gloves until you are working 25 feet from the two gloves. (You will need a longer leash as you add distance.)

The dog has been allowed to see both gloves and is seated facing neither glove.   *Ron Reagan*

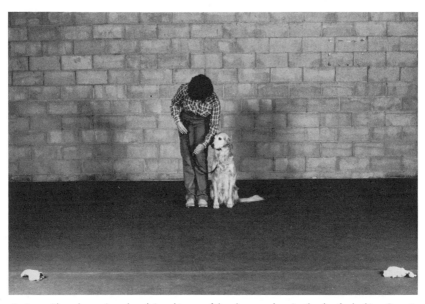

Facing neither glove, give a hand signal to one of the gloves and praise the dog for looking. Do not necessarily send him to retrieve the glove.   *Ron Reagan*

Step Five: Add Confusion

Add the center glove and shorten the distance. For the first week, do not send to the center glove at all. If the dog is not trying to pick it up when you send for gloves 1 and 3, you may start giving a signal to the center glove. Praise the dog for looking at the glove but don't send him to retrieve it. Extend your hand signal to glove 2 a little farther past the dog's head than the hand signal to the right and left gloves. This will become an added cue to your dog when you want him to retrieve glove 2 (center glove).

Up to this point you are facing glove 2 all of the time and have done no pivoting.

Step Six: Learn the Pivots

Pivots imply moving in place. All pivots are started on the right foot, which gives the dog a split second longer to notice which direction you are turning. Pivots should be done in two steps. If you are very uncoordinated, you may use three steps, and some people find that they cannot comfortably pivot left starting on their right foot.

Whenever you pivot to the right, which is asking the dog to move forward, use the "HEEL" command. When you pivot left, since the dog is required to back up, use a different command. "OFF" or "BACK" are commonly used, but any command is acceptable as long as it has no other meaning.

To teach the pivots to the right, command "HEEL" and with the heels of your shoes touching, move your right foot 45 degrees to the right. Then move your left foot into place next to it. The same procedure is used for the about turn except that you move your right foot 180 degrees to the right.

The pivot to the left requires a little more work as you teach the dog to back up, out of your way, as you pivot left into him. Begin by placing your right foot directly in front of the dog's left paw as he sits at Heel. Now command "OFF" or "BACK" as you pull the dog up and back and bring your left knee through the space where the dog was sitting and up to join your right foot. It is natural for you to trip over the dog the first few times, but eventually the dog learns to jump out of your way.

If your dog resists backing up, use a preliminary exercise of circling to the left. Each time, you circle tighter and tighter until you are pivoting in place. By holding the dog in place and commanding "BACK" or "OFF," the dog is coaxed into moving his body properly. Many breeds, especially Shelties and Collies, prefer to walk in a circle instead of backing up. Walking a small circle is not always penalized, but some judges deduct points because the dog has moved out of Heel position. To help your dog learn to back up or jump back, hold a jump stick in your left hand, parallel to your leg but on the side of the dog farthest from you. Begin with a sit at heel and your stick positioned. As you command "BACK," hold the dog's head with the leash in your right hand against your left leg. When the dog attempts to move his rump away from your left leg, prevent this with the stick. Since you are moving into the dog, he must move somewhere and since he is not permitted to circle, his only alternative is to back up in place.

To pivot to glove 1, pivot to the right. To pivot to glove 3, pivot left. To pivot to glove 2, it makes more sense to go left, unless you find it more difficult to get your dog to move backwards, in which case you may go to glove 2 by pivoting right. It makes more sense to go to glove 2 via glove 3 (left) because as you pivot the dog sees glove 3. If the dog was to focus on glove 3, you might be able to block his vision of it with your left hand giving the glove signal.

Step Seven: Add Pivots

Add your pivots and pivot to the glove you are sending the dog to. Continue to work pivots separately as well and incorporate them into your heeling work. Rotate sending the dog for all different gloves.

Step Eight: Proofing

Practice pivoting to one glove and sending the dog to another. Be careful when you do this that you are not blocking the dog's vision with your body. If necessary, step back out of the dog's sight line before giving the hand signal.

Tempt the dog to be wrong by moving glove 2 closer to the dog and then sending the dog to 1 and 3. Then reverse this and move gloves 1 and 3 closer and send to glove 2.

Use brown gloves on black mats or white gloves in the snow to teach the dog to follow your signal and take a line regardless of whether the dog sees the glove or not.

Try using five gloves instead of three. Be sure to give a careful signal.

What If the Dog Goes to the Wrong Glove?

If the dog is in the learning stages and is on a long line and heads for the wrong glove, prevent the dog from getting it by holding back the line (do not snap). Start over and if necessary walk out to the correct glove with your hand signal.

If the dog is working off leash and retrieves the wrong glove, say nothing. Stay in the bent over signal-giving position. Let the dog pick up the wrong glove. As he turns to come back to you, he will see you in the bent position and will know something is wrong. Let him be embarrassed for a few seconds and then stand up and slowly walk to the dog and remove the

Left—To help a dog learn to pivot backwards a jump stick is held in the left hand. *Right*—As you command "BACK," hold the leash in your right hand against your left leg. When the dog attempts to move his rump away from your left leg, prevent this by blocking his movement with the stick.

Ron Reagan

Proofing gloves by turning the dog to face a glove and then sending him with a clear signal to retrieve a different glove.

Ron Reagan

glove. Your silence is enough of a correction. Start over. If necessary, go back on the long line.

Never yell "NO" at a dog who is heading for the wrong glove. Never take a dog from one glove to another to "fix" the mistake. Once a mistake occurs, you cannot fix it, only redo it, hopefully with better understanding.

When the dog is retrieving nicely, unstuff the glove and practice the command "HOLD" with the glove. If you reach for the glove and say "HOLD," the dog should bite down and hold the glove. If you reach for the glove and command "OUT" or "GIVE," only then should the dog release the glove.

Problems

For dogs who insist on "killing" (shaking) the glove, fill the glove one third full with pebbles or fishing weights in the fingers of the glove so the dog ends up hitting himself in the head with the stones.

For the dog who has difficulty getting a good grip on the glove, starch the gloves when you wash them, crumple them up, and let them dry stiff and wrinkled. Practice with the dog retrieving the glove from under a chair leg where he will have to get a good grip to pull it out.

For the Ring

Be sure to present the judge with three CLEAN white work gloves before you enter the Utility ring.

Look to see where the gloves are being placed by the steward. Then be careful to pivot *to the glove*. Underpivoting or overpivoting is considered an aid to the dog and will result in points lost.

With small dogs you are permitted to get down to the dog's eye level (crouch), but you may not put your knee on the floor. The knee on the floor is considered an aid in direction to the dog.

41

Ready to Start Jumping?

OBEDIENCE is both an intellectual and physical sport for the canine participant. Before you can attempt to get a dog to jump hurdles 1½ times his height at the withers he must, like any athlete, be conditioned.

Top obedience dogs are lean and well muscled. Their trainers work hard to keep them physically fit to work obedience. Low jumping, running, and swimming are used to condition dogs.

Before a dog should be commanded to do any "high" jumping, he should be physically fit and sound. A hip x-ray will assure the trainer that the dog is not in pain when jumping and will give the trainer the confidence to insist on a jump response.

I like introducing young puppies to very low jumps. The pup is never commanded but rather encouraged to jump over something so small it is in no way damaging to his growing bones. A bar jump resting on paper cups is a good beginning. By exposing puppies to jumping, we avoid anxiety later on as the dogs recognize a jump from their early experiences.

Never ask your dog to jump on a slick surface where he might hurt himself. Remember, you and he are a team and both members of the team must trust each other. To put a dog in a potentially dangerous situation breaks down trust and the bond you are working to form. By the way, long, wet grass can be as slick as a shiny tile surface.

For a dog to be a good, easy jumper, he must have a balanced structure and a confident attitude. Most jumping problems are a combination of poor structure and insecurity. I have seen very poorly built dogs, even dysplastic dogs, appear to be excellent jumpers because they had a positive, enthusiastic, secure attitude about jumping. As a trainer you cannot change structure (although you can search for it in a puppy), but you can work on developing a good jumping attitude by starting the dog young and keeping it easy and fun.

What About Jump Sticks?

Jump sticks are black and white dowels which simulate bar jumps.

They can be an aid or a hindrance in teaching jumping. If you choose to use a jump stick, be careful to keep it stationary when commanding a dog to jump it. If you move the stick as the dog jumps, you confuse the dog's sense of timing.

The jump stick can be successfully used to teach a dog to kick out after he jumps so as not to "tick" the jump. When using it to teach "clean jumping," have someone who understands the procedure hold the stick just behind the high or bar jump and lift up on the stick as the dog's hind legs clear the top of the jump. Be careful not to overdo a good thing or you will soon be teaching your dog to somersault!

Signs of Jumping Problems

Some dogs are naturally, instinctively good jumpers—others are not. As a trainer it is important that you detect early signs of jumping problems. While it is true that dogs have different styles of jumping (some tuck and kick, others extend), certain movements are signs of a problem.

A good jumping dog approaches a jump aggressively and smoothly. *Stutter-stepping* in front of a jump means something is wrong. A dog will stutter-step for different reasons. He might have trouble judging or seeing the height of the jump and by stutter-stepping in front of it he buys time to decide how high to jump. A dog who is afraid to jump stutter-steps because he is trying to put it off until the last possible minute. While stutter-stepping, he is searching for the courage to commit to the jump. At the first signs of stutter-stepping, lower the jump and back up in your training to build the dog's confidence. It would also be advisable to get the dog's eyes examined by a veterinary ophthalmologist who has the equipment to check for eye diseases like PRA (Progressive Retinal Atrophy) and for problems with depth perception.

Another sign of jump trouble is when the dog clears the jump but in order to do so he twists his rear as he goes over the jump. A twisted rear movement means the dog is straining to clear the jump. He might lack muscle tone, be built poorly for jumping or may just be getting tired and should be rested. Do not raise the height of the jump until he has stopped twisting to clear the jump.

Play Jumping

The concept of "play jumping" was first explained to me by Cherie Berger of Meadowpond Goldens. It's a technique used to help teach jumping as well as to relieve stress associated with jumping problems. Most jumping problems start because the dog, for whatever reason, hits a jump and becomes reluctant to jump. The more the dog worries about the jump, the more tense he becomes, the less he is able to jump. It's a difficult problem to solve because it tends to become a cycle which may be difficult to break.

One way to break the cycle is to avoid jumping the dog for a week or more. This may sound contradictory since with most problems I advise causing the problem and working past it. Because stress makes jumping worse, it is not always the best approach to meet jumping problems head-on. After a week or more of not jumping, much of the stress associated with the exercise has dissipated, simply because of time. When you begin again to cope with the problem, try "play jumping."

To "play jump" your dog, set the jump at what was once a comfortable height for the dog. Do not put the dog on a Stay and avoid any formal commands. Go out with your dog and simply request "Jump for me." Encourage by running with the dog, tapping the jump or throwing a toy over the jump. If the dog chooses not to jump, there is no correction since you did not command him, you only asked him. Sometimes it takes as many as three sessions before the dog relaxes enough from the absence of pressure to attempt the jump. The dog may jump from any side and at any angle. Failure to jump is ignored. When the dog regains his confidence, you can go back to formal commands.

Play jumping helps the dog learn timing and teaches him to cope with various angles of jumping while avoiding stress.

Food rewards (tidbits) can also be used successfully to relieve the stress caused by anxiety over jumps.

42

Teaching the High and Bar Jumps

PREREQUISITES: Before teaching the high jump, or solid jump as it is sometimes called, the dog should be able to perform the following exercises:

1. Off-leash Novice recall of 35 feet.
2. Off-leash Novice sit-stay at 35 feet.
3. Pick up a dumbbell off the floor in front of him on command. (If you still need to correct the dog for not retrieving [ear-pinch] occasionally, it is acceptable to do so for this level of training.)

Prepare Yourself:

1. Build or purchase a high jump at least four feet wide. Make sure it is painted white. A board or table leaf covered with a white sheet will suffice temporarily. Understand that it is unfair to only jump a dog once a week at school, so you will have to arrange something for him to jump at home in practice.
2. Measure your dog while standing at the withers. (His head need *not* be held high, which tends to raise his withers!) Compute 1½ times this height (including fractions) and then round the number off to the nearest, lower even number. The result of your calculation is the height your dog will *eventually* have to jump according to current AKC regulations. (A few breeds are only required to jump once their height; these are listed in Chapter 4, Section 10, of the AKC *Obedience Regulations* booklet.)
3. To begin, set your jump to approximately 1/3 the height your dog will eventually jump, or lower if *you* cannot jump the other height or if your dog has never jumped before.

CAUTION!

1. Do not pull or snap *UP* on a leash to encourage a dog to jump. Dogs do not jump like elevators!! If any correction is used, it is always a snap *forward* to start the dog moving.
2. If a dog first learning to jump hits the jump, cheer anyway. You do not want to upset the dog so much that he doesn't want to try again. You encourage the *effort,* even if a mistake is made along the way.
3. Concentrate on achieving confidence and good jumping form. Do not expect a dog to jump his required full height before he has had from four to eight months of training. The specific interval will depend on the dog, his age and how often you train. When increasing height, raise the height one or two inches at a time. To make the jump only one inch higher, use a spacer if you do not have a 1-inch board.
4. Make sure your dog is in good physical health, good muscular condition, is not overweight, has short nails and does not have any disabilities such as hip dysplasia or cataracts. Some dogs can overcome these disabilities, but you as the trainer must be aware of them and train accordingly.
5. Do not jump a dog that has just eaten, has not had time to limber up with movement or is three or more weeks pregnant.
6. You cannot *force* a dog to jump, so don't try.
7. Be careful not to jump a dog to exhaustion when trying to work out a problem.
8. Most poor jumpers are insecure or frightened. Their owners were undoubtedly impatient. When in doubt as to how to help your dog overcome his insecurity or fear, LOWER THE JUMP.
9. There is a considerable difference to a dog between being able to see and not being able to see over what he is jumping. At the height where the dog can no longer see over the jump and is jumping on faith, you will need to take your time and let the dog gain his confidence. Most Open A dogs believe monsters lurk on the other side of the high jump.
10. Dogs that approach a jump so fast that they are not thinking or timing the jump must be slowed down before raising the height of the jump. You can accomplish this by having the dog jump multiple jumps at lower heights. This "in and out" jumping helps a dog learn timing.
11. Dogs have different jumping styles, even within the same breed. Usually dogs will tuck and then kick or extend their hind legs. Do not try to change the way a dog jumps, but if you have a lazy

jumper, you can encourage him to tuck tighter or extend higher with the use of a jump stick lifted as the dog goes over the jump.

12. It is not advisable to jump a dog over more than 16 inches with a leash dragging. The leash inhibits the dog's jumping ability. The less the leash is used, the more fluid jumping will become.

Steps to Teach tne High Jump and Bar Jump:

1. Have the dog on leash in Heel position. The leash should be loose but should not allow the dog to get further than six inches from your side. The only tension on the leash is between the dog and you. Sit the dog next to you about 15 feet in front of a high jump or bar jump set at 1/3 the full height. Command the dog to "HUP" (not "Heel") and proceed at a brisk but controlled pace towards the high jump. Head for the jump so that the dog is aimed at the center of the jump. Try not to slow down at all. Praise the dog as soon as he is *over* the jump. After landing, continue walking in a straight line until about 15 feet past the jump. Then, if you like, you can turn around and jump from the other side. It is important that the dog hears the "HUP" command *before* he starts moving. You will know when the dog understands because he will start to forge out ahead of you towards the jump. For the bar jump, use the command "BAR." By having different commands for the high jump and the bar jump, directed jumping will be less confusing.

2. When the dog is jumping confidently and forging ahead of you, take the leash off and do the same as above off leash. Do not worry if the dog moves out of Heel position. You never told him to heel! If the dog tries to go around the jump, let him, and then put the leash back on and go with him again. When the dog will jump with you off leash, he is confident at this height and is ready to progress.

3. Sit the dog off leash about six feet in front of the jump (closer if the dog is smaller). Leave the dog on a stay, and walk over the jump to the other side; turn and face the dog. With your entire hand, point to the top of the jump. Tap the jump if necessary to get the dog's attention. When you have the dog's attention, command "HUP" or "BAR" and back up. If the dog anticipates the jump before you command him to, praise anyway and next time do *not* tap the jump. If the dog tries to come around the jump, set him closer to the jump and repeat the tapping of the jump. If he still goes around, go back to Step 2 and, if necessary, Step 1. The only command the dog hears is "HUP" or "BAR" and he is only to hear it one time. The dog is never stopped or corrected for coming around the jump in the learning stages. When a mistake occurs, praise is withheld. Dogs learn by trial and error and must not be afraid to be wrong.

195

By using two bars on the bar jump you can help the dog visualize the height of the jump more easily.

Ron Reagan

Point out the high jump to the dog.

Ron Reagan

The hand signal to jump becomes the palm of your hand.

Ron Reagan

4. Practice heeling the dog with the dumbbell in his mouth. If at any time the dog drops the dumbbell, *he* is to pick it up with an ear-pinch correction from you. Repeat Step 1 now, with the dumbbell in the dog's mouth. Then go on and repeat Steps 2 and 3 with the dumbbell in the dog's mouth. Yes, the dog can jump a bar jump with a dumbbell. In fact, it is a good idea to use the retrieve over the bar as often as the retrieve over the high jump in preparation for Utility.

5. More dogs tend to go around the jump after having picked up the dumbbell than on the way out to retrieve over the jump. For this reason, we first work on the *return* with the dumbbell before we begin the retrieve over the high jump. Sit the dog at various points on the far side of the jump. Give him the dumbbell. Return by stepping over the jump. Turn and point to the jump. Now command "HUP" or "BAR." This should be done at all various angles until the dog has no doubt that regardless of what he is facing, when he hears a jump command, he is to return over either the high or bar jump. (The jump is still 1/3 the full height as in the beginning.)

6. Now you are ready to begin the *retrieve* over the jump. Take the jump down to eight inches. (If you do not have a full distance retrieve on the flat yet, do not attempt this!) Put the dog on a 6-foot leash. Command the dog to "STAY" and toss the dumbbell about three feet to the other side of the 8-inch high jump. Now command the dog to "HUP"; when the dog reaches the other side, command "TAKE IT," then again command "HUP" and finally command "SIT." The jumping often excites the dog, and he may start to mouth, or chew the dumbbell. If he does, command "HOLD" and enforce your command with a brief squeeze on his muzzle. The retrieve over the high jump is really a multiple of exercises, and initially you are cueing the dog every step of the way. Eventually, because dogs anticipate, you will simply say the first "HUP" and the dog will do the following parts of the exercise on his own. Remove the leash and gradually raise the height of the jump. Begin "proofing" the dog as described below.

7. Gradually you will raise the height of the jump. The more gradual, the better. If you work the dog every day, two inches per week is the fastest you should go. When the dog has retrieved successfully seven days at the new height, you may raise the height. Each time you do so, have the dog jump first without the dumbbell as in Step 3. When the dog is comfortable at the height, then build the exercise back up to Step 6. (Except that the dog is off leash after 16 inches of jump height.)

Proofing the Dog on the High Jump

Proofing begins at the low heights and continues through the training process up to the full height of the jump.

ANGLE THROWS—Since you can never be sure that the dumbbell will land and remain exactly opposite you on the other side of the jump, you should intentionally throw it off to one side to teach the dog that if you say "HUP," he should jump (even if he can see the dumbbell). Beginning this at low height helps the dog learn the concept of the exercise, when he can jump more often without getting tired.

STRANGE HIGH JUMPS—One high jump does not always look the same as another to a dog, yet he must have faith and jump them all. Practice jumping different jumps, and the same jumps in different places. Put a jacket over the jump, put flowers or balloons on the end of the jump, anything that might appear strange to the dog, and then enforce your command "HUP" until nothing frightens or spooks the dog. It is not uncommon to have shadows on a jump in a ring spook a dog. Proof to avoid this problem.

RETRIEVE ON FLAT AND HIGH CONFUSION—Once the dog has learned the high jump, there is a stage he will go through where he thinks that any time he sees a jump he is to jump it. Practice doing a retrieve on the flat next to the high jump. Your command here is "TAKE IT," not "HUP." We are teaching the dog at this point to listen to what we say, not to do what he thinks comes next. A good way to improve the dog's listening ability is to sit the dog in front of the jump, toss the dumbbell, then (with dog on lead or pull-tab) command "HEEL" and turn away from the jump. The dog will eventually learn to listen, which will help the high-flat confusion. Never yell "NO" if the dog is taking the jump when he shouldn't. Simply withhold praise and repeat the exercise, but this time stand where it would be too sharp an angle for the dog to jump. *Help* the dog by motioning with your hands. Do not correct him for what is only honest confusion!

IN AND OUT JUMPING—Place two high jumps approximately 12 feet apart and throw the dumbbell over both of them. Then command "HUP" and "HUP" again for the second jump. If a dog will jump over two jumps to retrieve a dumbbell, he is unlikely to go around *one*. This is also a good exercise to improve a dog's timing and build confidence.

This chapter explains the procedure for teaching the high jump. It does not deal with what to do if the dog does not give you the desired response. Each dog is different and each correction is based on the reason why the dog didn't perform. Keep in mind that you should not *correct* confusion or a dog which has not learned the exercise yet. You can only correct distraction or a dog that feels it has a choice. Learn to read your dog's reactions.

For a dog who does not jump because he is *afraid,* lower the jump.

If the dog does not jump because he is confused, help him by pointing to the jump and/or standing closer and encouraging.

If the dog is distracted, correct him, possibly with a lead snap towards you over a low (16″) jump.

If the dog is not jumping because he feels he has a choice, gently lift him (you might need a helper) and toss him carefully over the jump and praise him. Be sure you are very calm and controlled throughout this procedure. "Sweetheart," you might say, "you can do this on your own or I will do it to you, but one way or another you are going over that jump!" Your objective is to be consistent and deliberate and not to upset or frighten the dog. Most dogs are so utterly embarrassed when this happens that they willingly jump on their own the next time.

43

Directed Jumping

THE PURPOSE of directed jumping is to teach the dog to take a designated jump on command and/or hand signal from the handler.

This method assumes that the dog is familiar with both the high jump and bar jump from the Open jumping work done earlier in training.

Before you begin, you will need two bar jumps and two high jumps.

1. Begin by setting either the two high jumps or the two bar jumps approximately two feet apart, side by side. By using the same jumps, the only variable you introduce is the directional hand signal.

2. Position the dog in the middle of the two jumps, about eight feet back from them. Position yourself eight feet away from the jumps.

3. Learn how to give a clear signal. The signal begins as you turn your palm to face the dog while your arm still hangs at your side. (An experienced dog already knows which jump to take!) Now *slowly* and *smoothly* raise your arm, fingers together and palm facing the dog, up and slightly forward until it points to a jump. Your command for the dog to jump should be given towards the end of your hand signal, when the dog is sure which way to go. Flashed signals and rushed commands only lead to mistakes. In the ring you will not be permitted to lean into a signal or turn your head to indicate which jump, but when teaching the exercise you may begin by using some "body English" if necessary.

4. To begin teaching the exercise, leave your dog and walk over one of the jumps as you go to the other side. (If you walk between the jumps, the dog is likely to follow you.) Turn to face the dog and give a slow, smooth signal to the jump you just walked over. Command the dog to jump. If he sits there, leave your hand signal up as you walk over and tap the jump with the hand signal. This should stimulate him to jump as you used the tap to first teach him to go over these jumps. If not, you may encourage him as you tap.

Begin by setting two of the same kind of jumps a few feet apart. To avoid having the dog come between the jumps, block the opening with a barrier. *Ron Reagan*

The dog should see the palm of your hand through the middle of the correct jump. *Ron Reagan*

Alternate jumps and sides. Sometimes use high jumps, sometimes bars. If at any time the dog takes the wrong jump, say nothing and leave your hand signal up. When the dog lands and sees your arm still up, he will know something is wrong. In the teaching stage, this is enough of a correction. Start over and see if he doesn't pay closer attention.

5. Gradually spread the distance between the jump and stop going over a jump on your way to the other side. As you widen the picture, move the jumps apart as you back the dog and yourself away from center.

6. When the dog is secure at full distance, use one of each jump.

Proofing the Exercise

In the ring the jumps will be 18-20 feet apart. A new Utility dog often doesn't know how to locate the jumps. You can proof against this problem by practicing with jumps 25-30 feet apart.

Have someone throw a ball or some other distraction in front of your dog before he jumps.

Have someone tap a jump and then you send the dog over a different jump. This teaches the dog to focus his attention on you and avoid extraneous movements.

Try leaning one way and sending the dog over the other jump. Is he really responding to the signal?

Work to different backgrounds and in different locations.

Stand with your back to your dog and give a hand signal! (Make sure your palm still faces the dog.) This will determine if the dog really understands the concept of a signalled jump or if he is getting extra cues from your face.

Give signals only to direct the dog.

If you are really brave, try sending the dog on verbal commands only. (Since each jump has a different command, this is possible!)

44

Teaching the Broad Jump

THE BROAD JUMP exercise is taught in a step-by-step process. It is absolutely imperative that each step be performed successfully before the next step is attempted. Every dog learns at a different rate. Do not compare your dog's progress; learn at your own rate.

1. Set up the bar jump, with the bar at a low height; add two boards from the broad jump, placing one directly in front of the bar and the other directly behind it (one board under the bar is used for extremely small dogs). Walk briskly with the dog over the boards on leash. Do not snap up on the leash at any time as this will throw the dog off balance. Introduce the dog to the command OVER by commanding, "Fido, OVER!" *before* you start for the jump. The dog should be told what he is being asked to do before he begins moving. If the dog makes any attempt to walk the boards, set them up on end, put chicken wire over them, or raise them by setting them up on tuna cans! Now take the leash off and again walk with the dog over the jump.

2. Leave your dog on a sit stay and walk to the opposite side of the broad jump. With the bar jump, and possibly chicken wire, over the jump, point to the bar with your hand to show the dog what you want and then give the command "Fido, OVER." You are now having the dog move towards you over the jump until he is confident. Remember, the command is "Fido, OVER!" not "COME." If the dog heads around the jump, put up a barrier so he can't, or snap him toward you on leash before he can start going around, or go back to Step 1.

3. Work until the dog will do a recall on the command "OVER" (not "COME") over the jump off leash without trying to go around or walk the jump. (Bar jump is still over the broad jump.)

4. Gradually spread the two broad jump boards to full distance. (This may take days or weeks.) The bar jump is still over the center

Set up the bar jump at a low height and add two boards from the broad jump, one directly in front of the bar and the other directly behind.   *Ron Reagan*

Should the dog step between the boards and the bar jump, put chicken wire on the floor.   *Ron Reagan*

Point to the bar with your hand to show the dog that you want him to jump.
Ron Reagan

Gradually spread the two boards to full distance.   *Ron Reagan*

Remove the bar jump uprights gradually. Eventually the bar is resting on the floor. Chicken wire may be necessary at this point.
Ron Reagan

Remove the bar jump totally.
Leave the wire if necessary.
Ron Reagan

of the jump. If at any time the dog steps between the boards and the bar jump, put chicken wire on the floor.

If your dog is not bothered by stepping in chicken wire, you can try sticky-side-up contact paper or double-faced tape. For very large dogs, dig a ditch, fill it with ice and then mark it with two broad jump boards!

Once the dog is consistently and confidently jumping full distance (and without using chicken wire), remove the bar jump and proceed to Step 5. You may need to replace the chicken wire temporarily if the dog steps between the boards; you may even need to shorten the distance between the boards initially. Lay the bar jump on the ground before removing it totally. Remove the uprights of the bar jump gradually as these help the dog to focus his attention to the other side of the jump.

The only time a leash helps with a broad jump problem is when the dog refuses to attempt the jump, but pulling a dog on a line will not cause him to jump. He can just as easily trot through it.

The first and last boards of the broad jump are the ones the dog must learn to focus on if he is to take off and land properly. To avoid confusion, we omit the middle boards until the dog has mastered the concept of jumping from the first to the last board.

5. Do a recall over the jump but stand with your left shoulder facing the dog as you command "OVER." This gets the dog used to having you give him the command as you stand sideways, which is eventually what he will see. As the dog reaches you, make a 90 degree pivot to the right, away from the dog. This will start to teach the dog to turn and come in to you. Guide the dog around and into a straight sit front. (You do not move, only pivot.)

Pivot 90°

6. Continue as above until you can do a recall over the jump off leash with boards spread to full distance. Continue to pivot 180 degrees after the dog lands to teach him to turn.

7. Gradually work your way around to the side of the jump. In a ring situation you will want to stand almost even with the last board of the broad jump (so that your body helps the dog judge the length of the jump) and according to the rule book, *"with your toes about two feet from the jump." The handler shall change his position by executing a right-angle turn while the dog is in mid-air, but shall remain in the same spot."* This turn is the same as a pivot, started on the right foot. By keeping your heels touching, you will be sure not to move out of position.

YOU - start here   (Pivot 90° to your
YOU - move to here   right as dog is in
YOU - then to here   mid-air.)

8. When you are actually in line with the jump, put up a gate or some barrier to prevent the dog from turning too soon.

barrier   (You pivot 90° to your
YOU   right when dog is in
mid-air.)

9. Now try standing in a normal position at the side of the jump. With the barrier in place, the dog should use up his momentum before he turns tightly to come in to you.

DOG

barrier   (You pivot 90° to your
YOU   right when dog is in
mid-air.)

As the dog turns the corner of the barrier, command "COME" and encourage a brisk front. You may even run backwards. Should the dog attempt to come straight to you now that you are at the side, put up another barrier on his right before the jump, and if necessary to the side of the jump.

DOG

barrier   barrier   barrier
YOU

When you are actually in line with the jump, put up a gate or barrier to prevent the dog from turning too soon. *Ron Reagan*

Gradually work your way around the barrier to the side of the jump. *Ron Reagan*

A dog who understands the Broad Jump exercise will jump on command from the first board to the last board, with no boards in the middle and the handler at the side of the jump. *Ron Reagan*

10. Add the center board(s) if your dog is required to jump more than two. The dog should have no problems with this if jumping confidently the full distance using only two boards.
11. Remove the barrier, but be ready to run in towards the dog if he starts to turn too quickly. Dogs that turn too quickly use up their momentum with a sweeping wide circle.

YOU — Run into dog if he turns too soon.

YOU WRONG

12. When dog is doing a nice broad jump, from time to time still run towards the front of the jump. If the dog never knows when you're going to run, he will never cut the corner!
13. If dog is slow in coming in to front, take off running away after you command him to "COME."

Proofing

Do the broad jump in many different places.

Face the dog *away* from the jump and command him "OVER."

Start the dog from a down position.

Have someone else try to distract the dog as he is waiting for the command to jump.

45

Teaching Utility Hand Signals

THE STAY SIGNAL is given with your left hand, palm facing the dog, in front of his eyes.

To teach the stay signal, simply use it with the verbal command and then enforce the stay.

The heel signal is given with the left hand in a scooping forward motion which should pass both of the dog's eyes. (He has two, so use both!)

To teach the heel signal, hold the dog on a snug leash. Give the hand signal as you say "HEEL" and *then* step forward on your left leg. After one or two times, give the heel signal only, say nothing, and then step forward on your left foot. Praise! A common mistake made in the utility ring is that the handler gives the hand signal to heel at the *same time* that he steps off with his left foot. This often causes a lag. Just as you should give a verbal "HEEL" *before* you move, the dog should receive a hand signal to heel *before* you move.

The come signal is taught when learning the karate chop recall. It is modified slightly in Utility as you bring your right arm out to your side away from your body before you bring it in and slap the leash for a correction (if the dog didn't respond). In beginners the signal was more of an up-and-down motion to give the beginner more leverage on the leash. Whenever possible, we keep signals away from our body where they are more visible. Make sure your hand ends up pointing front at the completion of your signal. This is "legal cheating" where you have an opportunity to point out front in the ring just before the dog does a recall!

The drop or down signal is given with the right arm and is the same as for the drop on recall. (See Chapter 34.) Handlers either use the entire "windmill" signal or shorten it to a smooth up-and-down motion with the right palm clearly facing the dog.

The sit signal is perhaps the most difficult to teach. We want the dog to sit by bringing his front feet up and back so as not to move himself out of position. The signal is given with the left hand, palm facing the dog.

Put the dog in a crouched down on leash directly in front of you. Command "SIT" as you slide your left hand, palm facing the dog, past both

The Stay Signal. *Ron Reagan*

The Recall Signal. Notice that the handler's palm is facing the dog before it hits the leash and ends up pointing to the front position. *Julia Brown*

Completion of the Recall Signal. Notice that the hand ends up at the midpoint of the handler's body, reinforcing the "front" concept. *Ron Reagan*

The Drop Signal.   *Ron Reagan*

Completion of the Drop Signal. Notice that the hand comes down onto the dog's shoulders so that at no time does the dog ever see the back of the hand.

Ron Reagan

of his eyes while pulling back on the leash with your right hand, which allows you to pull the dog up into a sit as you bring the *side* of your right sneaker gently against his chest. Eventually, as the dog sees your left palm moving up and away from your body, he will "pop" up into a sit away from you as he avoids the sneaker against his chest.

For small dogs, teach this on a table and your hand is usually enough to assure the dog moves his front feet back to his rear.

The stand signal is given with the right hand, palm facing the dog. You raise your right hand over the dog's eyes (encouraging him to look up) and stop his motion by first touching his stifle with your left hand. Initially you may use a verbal command. For small dogs, use the leash looped under the dog's stomach to stand him as the signal is given.

The finish signal is done with either the right or the left hand, depending on whether your dog has learned to finish to the right or left. To teach the finish signal, gather the leash under the hand giving the signal (your thumb can hold the lead as your hand remains flat). At first give the verbal command as you move your hand and the leash. Eventually move just your hand and the leash, which will automatically help the dog.

In general, signals should be clear, smooth, consistent and never flashed. Be conscious that your palm faces the dog whenever possible, which adds to the visibility of your signal from a distance. Sloppy signals are often cause for a dog's mistake. By using the left hand for heel, the right hand for stand, the left for stay, the right for down, the left for sit and the right for come, we are always alternating hands, which helps to keep the signals distinct.

I recommend wearing a plaid or print long-sleeve shirt with contrasting colors and some white to give your dog the best chance to see your arms move at a distance. This theory came about one day in New York as I watched two flags flapping in the wind. One flag was an American Flag and the other one was all white except for a round insignia in the center. By watching the flags high above move in the wind, I realized that the contrasting colors of the American flag made its movement much clearer than that of the almost completely white flag. Since then I have always worn prints (usually plaids with some white) in the Utility ring and try to contrast with the background as much as possible. If you don't know what the background will be, bring two shirts!

Good handlers quickly master the act of giving clear, consistent signals away from their bodies with palms facing the dog. Practicing in front of a mirror helps. However, most mistakes made in the Utility signal exercise are the result of a lack of attention on the part of the dog. In practice, if your dog looks off, give him a clear signal, followed by the signal's correction if he misses it. You will never develop dog attention if you are willing to wait for the dog to look back or by saying "Watch me," thus doing his work for him. Signals are taught on leash, in close, and the

The Sit Signal. The left hand, palm facing the dog, slides up the leash, past the dog's eyes and off to the left of the handler.   *Ron Reagan*

The handler's foot steps towards the dog encouraging him to pull his front feet back into a sit. For the resistant dog, the side of the handler's foot taps the dog in the chest to encourage him to pull his front feet back into a sitting position.   *Ron Reagan*

The Stand Signal. Notice that the right hand giving the signal is above the dog's head. This encourages the dog to look up and thus stand with his head high. The right hand and the right foot are moved at the same time.

Ron Reagan

Using the leash to teach the small dog the Stand Signal.

Ron Reagan

216

To teach the Finish Signal, gather the leash under the thumb of your right hand.
Julia Brown

The Finish Signal from the dog's point of view.
Ron Reagan

217

goal after the dog learns the various signals is to try to distract the dog so that he learns what happens if he looks off. Good distractions include: food, toys, people waving hands, someone petting the dog or standing over the dog. When the dog ignores all distractions, you may start to increase your distance. If the dog misses the signal and is corrected when he looks off, it becomes to his advantage to watch you and you never have to tell him to!

Be sure to practice doing signals in all different orders to avoid patterning the exercise. Dogs learn the signals quickly; the attention training takes a little longer.

46

Go-Out

OF ALL THE EXERCISES in AKC obedience, the go-out is perhaps the most frustrating to teach and difficult to perfect. The reason for this is that the go-out exercise makes no sense. There is no intelligent animal that I know of who will at any time, other than in a Utility ring, charge in a straight line towards a brick wall or similar barrier. It would be as if you were in the driver's seat of a car and someone pointed you towards a stone wall and said, "Floor it!" All of your instincts would tell you to veer one way or the other in anticipation of a turn so as not to hit the wall head on. In other words, you would not be inclined to do a straight go-out either!

It is relatively easy to get a dog to run in a straight line towards open space. The field trainers do it all the time. While it has been said that the go-out is similar to a blind retrieve exercise in the field, I do not find much similarity at all. There is never anything in a ring for a dog to retrieve on a go-out, and blind retrieves in the field are not done toward barriers.

Aside from the fact that the go-out exercise makes no sense, its difficulty is increased as the sight picture of go-out in a ring is always changing. When you teach a dog to jump a high jump, you are assured of what the jump will look like in every ring. When you teach go-out, you must train for all different kinds of barriers (string, baby gates, walls, solid barriers, other fence-type structures) which makes the process take longer and frequently adds to the dog's confusion.

From what I am told, years ago in the sport of obedience the go-out was merely an exercise where the dog left his handler and went to the other side of the ring, approximately to the center. In fact, *approximate center* is still the wording used in the AKC regulations. No points were lost for a dog who was three feet off center. As training has improved and as our top working dogs have gotten so good that at times they are difficult to fault, the only way the judges can split the really top dogs is to pick apart go-outs. Now, if your dog isn't exactly in the middle of the ring, you can expect to lose points. What began as a reasonable exercise which made little sense is now a ridiculous exercise which makes *no* sense!

Since it is silly to teach a "thinking dog" a nonsensical exercise, we have changed the "go-out" exercise as it appears to the dog. "Go out" is no longer an action (verb) but rather a location (noun). From our dog's point of view, "go out" becomes a place in the ring that we want him to go to, similar to the English agility "go out" where the dog goes to a designated marked spot on the ground and lies down. Location, or target as it is sometimes referred to, became our choice of method because the only way a person could walk a straight line would be to line up two points and walk with these points remaining in line. For those of you who track or are planning to learn, this concept of lining up two points is basic. I have not yet found a way to teach a dog to line up two points, but it is possible to teach him to go to one point.

"Go-out" is divided into three separate teaching steps. It is important that when you are working on one step you do not worry that the dog is not doing another step.

The first concept to teach is that on the command "GO OUT" or "GO 'WAY" the dog is to leave your side. The easiest and most mechanical way to teach a dog to leave your side is to pull him away from you with the use of a pulley. The pulley gets the dog to leave your side in a matter of moments and avoids confusion of any kind. An alternative to using the pulley is to encourage the dog to go to a toy or food. I prefer using the pulley to using bribery because when a dog is going to food or a toy he is thinking about the food or toy and is not thinking about what he is doing. It is important that if you use a pulley you do not become concerned with the dog going straight since it is normal for a dog to avoid a line and arc away from it. With all breeds of dogs and all temperaments, I have never had to use a pulley for more than two sessions (5 to 15 minutes each time) to teach a dog to leave my side. One pulley at your training location serves all dogs.

The pulley may be set up so that it pulls the dog to a solid wall, or it may be nothing more than a person pulling a line through a gate. In either case, the person pulling the rope must be experienced enough to know when to pull, when to stop pulling, how to pull and what kind of collar to pull with. Sometimes steady pressure on a buckle collar is all that is needed, and sometimes jerks on a prong collar are what it takes initially to get a dog to leave your side.

The first few times the dog is pulled out, the handler should walk with him. With each successive attempt, the handler stops shorter and shorter and the dog goes further on his own.

The second concept is to teach the dog to go until you tell him to stop. This is accomplished with the use of a target. Begin with scissor gates and ring stanchions if the dog shows in your area ordinarily use scissor gates as rings. It stands to reason that if most of your shows use stakes and ropes, then that is what you would start with. Eventually you will want to accustom your dog to all kinds of barriers. Along with the scissor gates and stanchions, use two broad jump boards which will work to give the dog a

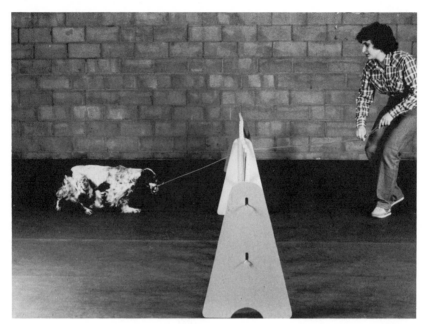

The pulley teaches the dog to leave the handler's side. A person pulling the dog out on a long line has the same effect. *Ron Reagan*

The broad jump boards make a guide that teaches the dog to turn tightly before sitting. *Ron Reagan*

221

place to go to and will get a tight turn and sit at the end of the go-out. Both the ring stanchion and the broad jump boards are targets. This is so that later, when you transfer the dog to different barriers and there is no stanchion, he still has the security of the boards.

To Teach "Go 'til I Tell You to Stop"

Begin by gathering the leash in your right hand, turn your body towards the dog slightly so he doesn't think you're heeling, give the command "GO OUT," and run with the dog, your right hand ahead of his face, between the broad jump board guides and gently make the dog touch the stanchion with his nose. A dog cannot understand the difference between two feet from the gate or four feet from the gate, but he does understand the difference between touching the stanchion versus not touching. In the future, any time the dog stops short, he will be corrected by being taken to the stanchion and will be made to touch it. In training, however, if the dog gets close enough to have touched the stanchion, we will accept it as close enough. In the ring, we will stop the dog just before the dog reaches the stanchion.

The final step is to teach the dog to run in a straight line. This is more difficult for some dogs than others. There are dogs who, because of structural faults, are not capable of walking in a straight line. Dogs who naturally "crab" must learn to compensate if they are to end up doing straight go-outs.

A dog will never understand an abstract concept like straight. So far I have been unable to teach a dog to line up two points in order to walk a straight line. The best I can do is teach the dog to focus his attention on a single point (target) ahead of him and pattern him to walk a straight line. A patterned straight line is accomplished by providing the dog with a chute. The chute might be two pieces of white clothesline (which will eventually become a darker color rope) if you work outdoors or a series of white fold-up rulers (easily transportable) if you work indoors.

Set up your chute, guides and target. Position the dog three feet outside the guides. Leave the dog and stand behind the gate, facing the dog. Point to the stanchion as you command the dog "GO OUT." Encourage the dog with body and voice if he is reluctant to move. After he will readily come to you at the stanchion, you are ready to go on. Sit the dog three feet in front of the guides. Leave the dog and go between the guides and show the dog the stanchion. Make sure he is looking and that you are not blocking his vision. As you return to the dog, command him to "GO OUT" and motion forward with your right arm just as a gesture that it's okay to leave your side. At this point, your right arm is merely gesturing to leave. As soon as the dog leaves confidently, eliminate the use of any hand signal. Follow slowly behind the dog, who will probably stop just short of the

Run with the dog with your right hand ahead of his face pointing to the stanchion. *Ron Reagan*

Gently make the dog touch
the stanchion with his nose.
Ron Reagan

The broad jump boards are a part of the total chute used to teach the dog to walk in a straight line.
Ron Reagan

If the dog gets up and comes to you when you point out the target (stanchion) let him and encourage him to touch it with his nose. For some dogs, your standing behind the stanchion is easier for the dog to see what you are pointing to.
Ron Reagan

stanchion. When he stops and looks bewildered, gently move his nose to touch the stanchion. Then command his name as you turn him *to the left* and command him to "SIT."

If the dog leaves your side but avoids the guides, gently guide him into them. For the first 50 times that you send the dog, make sure to point out the stanchion immediately before you send him. Most dogs naturally turn to the right. Dogs who turn to the left have an easier time with straight go-outs. The dog starts out on your left side and usually arcs away from the way he turns (like a bad driver who goes left to turn right). If the dog arcs to the right and *turns to the left,* he should end up right in front of you. You can teach your dog to turn left by guiding him to the left with the leash before you command "SIT."

This method of teaching go-out in no way makes use of any retrieve exercises, and a hand signal is not used. Therefore, the confusion often seen between gloves and go-outs is minimal. A dog seen going to a ring corner is not necessarily confused and looking for a glove. The dog goes back to the glove corner because he has lost his go-out target and doesn't know where else *to go.* I refer to this as a "lost go-out" as opposed to a case of "glove/go-out confusion."

To transfer the dog from the stanchion target to other targets, start back in close (five or six feet) to the new barrier. Put up your guides and chute. Point out the new target and start over. Gradually wean the dog off the guides and chute but always go back for reinforcements. Fold-up rulers eventually used as a guide are not easily seen from a distance so the dog is practically going on his own until he reaches the barrier and sees the rulers.

It is certainly fun to do go-outs to wide open space, and the dogs learn to like it and really pick up speed, but I find that it has little carry-over to a barrier ring situation.

The go-out exercise needs constant work since it is always changing. If you know ahead of time what barrier the dog will be sent to in the ring, practice to that kind of barrier the week before in training.

If a dog stops short, take him by the "dead ring" of the collar (on his two hind legs if necessary) and make him touch his nose to the stanchion.

Some dogs tend to walk back towards you before they sit. To prevent the "walk back," do not call your dog to you after the go-out in early training. This problem can be eliminated if you will quietly walk behind the dog as he goes out. When he turns to face you and starts to walk back, you will be there to enforce the sit. If the dog is too fast for you to get there in time to stop him, throw a rolled-up leash between you and him after you command "Fido, SIT."

Ideas for Proofing the Go-Out

It is important that your dog remain focused on the go-out target and

Point out the target. *Ron Reagan*

The guides are eventually reduced in size to small white folding rulers. *Ron Reagan*

The correction for a dog who chooses not to do a go out, or for one who is distracted, is to take him out on his hind legs until he touches the stanchion with his nose. Notice that the collar is not choking the dog. The collar is only used to lift the dog's front feet off the ground. *Ron Reagan*

not become distracted. This is accomplished by proofing. At any time that the dog loses his concentration and misses the go-out target, he is taken by the dead ring of the collar with only his hind legs touching the ground and made to touch the stanchion. He is then praised.

1. Have people and dogs standing and/or moving behind your barrier.
2. Have someone throw a ball or frisbee in front of the dog as he does the go-out. If he loses his concentration, correct him.
3. You throw a ball into a corner of the ring, then command, "GO OUT." If the dog heads for the ball, he is wrong.
4. Put white pieces of paper which might resemble gloves in the ring corners, then send your dog. If he heads for the corners, he is wrong.
5. Have someone try to distract your dog with noise, food, or by petting him just before you send him. And if he falls for any distraction, correct him!

47

Secrets of Showing

AS A TEAM, you and your dog will strive to give a sharp, neat, accurate performance and appearance in the ring. The appropriate dress can help you accomplish this.

Suggestions for Ladies

Pants suits or slacks with tops and sometimes even vests make good show wear. Make sure pants legs are not too flared as this might interfere with Heel position. Skirts and dresses are also acceptable, but if you haven't worked your dog in a skirt, don't start it at a show.

It is to your advantage to try to match the color of your clothes as closely as possible to the color of your dog. For example, it is very difficult to detect a crooked sit by a black dog sitting next to a black pants leg. Most dancing teams dress alike, so why not a dog and handler team? You may even choose to go as far as to dress incorporating your dog's breed or original purpose, e.g. wearing feathered earrings with field dogs, rhinestones with Pomeranians or Poodles, sheepskin vests with Border Collies, or red suspenders with Dalmatians! Your creative efforts may or may not be appreciated by the judge, but your overall performance will appear costumed to perfection.

Avoid wearing strange perfume, noisy jewelry or long belts where the ends swing freely as these might distract the dog. Never wear sunglasses in a ring. This frightens some dogs and besides, you need eye contact!

When showing outside, wear warm undergarments and plan to take your heavy coat off before going into the ring. The coat causes interference and covers Heel position and Front. If your hair is long and tends to fall in your face, tie it back. You don't want to be accused of a second command by unconsciously brushing hair out of your eyes.

Suggestions for Men

Comfortable sports clothes chosen to match the color of the dog are ideal for the obedience ring. Whenever possible, try to incorporate the purpose or origin theme of your dog's breed into your outfit to enhance your overall picture of teamwork. Slacks should permit freedom of movement without appearing baggy or ill-fitting. At no time should a sport jacket or suit jacket be worn in the obedience ring. While a neat, formal look is appreciated by some judges, a sport jacket does not benefit the dog. For one thing, you probably don't wear a jacket every time you work with the dog. Your dog has learned to judge "Front" and "Heel" position based on the contour of your body in the clothing you generally wear to train. Now is not the time to cover up front with a sport jacket! Should you feel that you would like a more formal appearance, a tie can be worn with or without a sleeveless sweater. Even bow ties have made a comeback into the obedience ring.

If you have trained your dog to focus "front" on a belt buckle, be sure the buckle is visible to the dog in the ring. Avoid pockets full of change and keys that might jingle as you do a fast. Both men and women should remember to wear comfortable shoes (the same color as the dog) regardless of costume choice. Make a point to practice heeling the dog in the shoes you plan to wear in the ring. Your footwork is always easier to control when the shoes you wear offer good side support.

Don't Forget the Dog

Your dog should be clean, brushed and groomed in keeping with his breed. You should be as proud of his appearance as his performance. Be sure there are no tags, ribbons or other attachments on your dog's choke chain before you take him in the ring as this is prohibited by the rules.

Remember, a good appearance doesn't make up for poor training, but a sloppy appearance can hurt the score of a well-trained dog.

When to Arrive at a Show

After you have entered a sanctioned obedience trial, you will receive in the mail a judging schedule and a number for your dog. Bring your schedule and entry pass to the show. You will know from the schedule how many dogs are in the class and how many dogs are supposed to show before yours. The schedule may also tell you if the class will break for lunch, when this break will be, and if the break is mandatory or up to the judge. Keep this in mind when figuring when you will most likely show. It is reasonable to estimate four minutes per dog in Novice, six minutes per dog in Open and eight minutes per dog in Utility. Of course, this will also depend on how many dogs show up and how fast the judge works! When figuring time of showing, include time for group exercises.

Try to get to the show at least an hour to an hour and a half before you might be in the ring. If there is bad weather on the day of the show, keep in mind that more dogs will be absent and be there earlier. The judge is not required to judge you if you are not there when he gets to your number.

What to Do When You Arrive at the Show

Leave your dog in the car (if it's not too hot) and take your blanket or crate, a water dish and water, chair, and any other equipment you have with you, and investigate the show setup. Locate your ring and "check in" with the steward. He or she will give you an armband that corresponds to your catalog number. You may also ask at this time if the judge plans to take a break and if so, when. Make sure to notice what number dog is in the ring and which dogs before you have picked up armbands, which indicates they are present. Locate a space to sit and watch your ring, but preferably *not* directly outside the ring. You do not want the dog looking for his blanket or other members of the family when he is in the ring.

Once settled, go get your dog. If you plan to show within the hour, exercise the dog. Then bring him into the show under control and let him get used to the surroundings. Do not let him sniff other dogs or people. You may walk with him but do not train him on the grounds as this is not permitted at a sanctioned show or match. Locate a place away from the show grounds where you can legally practice with your dog before the class. You may need a correction or two before you show, and this should not be done in public on the show grounds. The area considered show grounds should be mapped out in the premium list or catalog, or you can ask the show chairman what area is considered "show grounds."

It is important for you to watch what is happening in your ring. Familiarize yourself with the Heeling pattern and from what end of the ring the judge is doing the recalls and where the Figure 8 is to be done, etc. The same is true for Open and Utility exercises. Before you enter the ring, you should know where each exercise begins so you can get there without having to be told by the judge. Pay attention to difficult parts of the Heeling pattern but do not try to memorize the pattern as this might cause you to anticipate a command and lose points. A general idea that the judge is doing an "L"-shaped or a "T"-shaped pattern should be sufficient.

Things to be Aware of While in the Novice Ring

While you are not permitted to talk to the dog during an exercise other than the initial command, you may talk and praise him between the exercises. Ending an exercise the judge will always say, "Exercise finished." Before you begin an exercise the judge should ask, "Are you ready?" This will let you know when it is safe to talk to the dog, praise him, keep him "up" and demand attention.

In Novice, be sure to go no farther than six feet away from your dog on the stand for examination exercise. Six feet is two big steps. When returning to the dog on the stand exercise, be careful to return to the *Heel* position, i.e. even with the dog's head to shoulder. Failure to do this results in a point loss. When you stand your dog for the judge to examine, it is not wise to face him towards the entrance of the ring. No need to tempt him to leave! Be sure your dog is standing comfortably and squarely before you leave him and that your hands are not on the dog when you actually command "STAY."

On the heel on leash exercise, make sure your leash is loose. A loose leash should have the clasp at the end of the leash hanging down. Should you totally lose your dog on the heel off leash exercise, you may repeat the "HEEL" command. You will be penalized for a second command, but you will not forfeit the entire exercise if the dog recovers.

Make sure that your hands are directly by your sides when you call your dog on the recall exercise and that you do *not* move your head as this is considered a second command. The same is true for bending at the waist or for bending your knees. The dog must respond on voice or hand signal alone to the command "COME." All extraneous body movements may be considered an aid to the dog and be penalized accordingly.

In Novice you may gently guide the dog by placing your hand in the ring of the choke collar between exercises. Hopefully, if you are talking to the dog and if he is paying attention, this will not be necessary.

Be alert and at ringside for your group exercises. It is not the responsibility of the judge or stewards to find you. When you position your dog for the group stays, make sure he is not sitting on a crack in the mats or on an ant hill, if outdoors. Place your leash far enough behind your dog so that if he wags his tail he wouldn't hit the leash and scare himself. After you give the "STAY" command, place your arms behind your back and leave them there until the judge says "Exercise finished." Your dog is less likely to confuse the stay with the recall if your arms are positioned differently for each.

Things to be Aware of While in the Open Ring

Before you enter an Open or Utility ring, check to see that the jump heights are correct.

No guiding of the dog is permitted in the Open and Utility rings, so keep your hands off the dog except for praise.

Be careful not to add any extra body English (e.g. bending, bobbing head, etc.) to your recall and signal for the drop on recall. If you are using a verbal command to drop your dog, keep the tone sweet and the volume reasonable. Excessively loud commands may be penalized. If you are using a signal for the drop, be careful that it is a continuous motion. "Held signals" are penalized.

As a handler, it is your job to learn how to throw a dumbbell so that your dog has the advantage of retrieving in a straight line. If you practice and concentrate on where you want the dumbbell to land, you can perfect the art of dumbbell tossing.

For the high jump, position yourself so that you are standing where the dog is likely to return over the jump. This will help your front. Be sure to give your dog plenty of room to jump. While the rule book states a minimum of eight feet, you may stand back as far as the ring permits.

When positioning yourself at the broad jump, the rule book states you are to be two feet from the jump. Two feet is longer than you think. Learn to estimate two feet accurately.

Things to be Aware of While in the Utility Ring

Be sure you know where each exercise begins so that you can move quickly around the ring and give your dog the advantage of seeing the steward put the articles out and a chance for the dog to see the "go out" picture.

When the steward is placing the gloves out, look to see where they are. Then, be careful to pivot so that the dog is facing the correct glove. Under-pivoting or over-pivoting is considered an aid to the dog and is judged accordingly.

When preparing for the group stand for examination, take your time and make sure your dog is positioned comfortably.

If you plan to reuse your articles in the near future, mention to the stewards that you would like the scented articles kept separate from the others. Most stewards are happy to do this if they are aware that you prefer it.

What to Do as Your Class Is Ending

As you notice the last group of stays are being performed, wake your dog up, exercise him and get ready for a possible run-off. There is nothing more upsetting than to be caught off guard for a run-off. Since you are not the judge, if you qualify, prepare for a possible run-off.

What to Do After Your Class Has Ended

Shortly after a class is completed, the breakdown of the individual scores of each dog is posted by the superintendent's desk. It is often helpful to find out which exercises cost you the most points. Track down these posted scores so you will know what to work on. If you are displeased with your dog's performance, do not take it out on the dog. He only knows what you taught him or didn't teach him. View every show as a learning experience. There is always tomorrow. If you find that your dog does perfectly at home and blows it at a show, you probably need to work him in more varied places and proof harder. Keep in mind that every dog, even the best, will occasionally "blow it." To err is canine!

Understanding Sportsmanship

The way competition works:

If there is to be a winner, there must be a loser. It is easier to be a winner than to accept defeat graciously.

Your dog should work for *you,* and *you* should be his strictest critic. Sometimes you will be very pleased with your dog's performance and your score will not reflect your opinion. Sometimes you will be unhappy with your dog's performance and you will end up a winner. Actually, it is quite rare that both you and the judge will agree on the dog's caliber of work! You cannot train your dog to please every judge, only to please yourself. When you choose to show under a judge, you are asking for that judge's opinion. Accept the score with the understanding that it is only one person's opinion. If you do not like a particular judge's opinion of your dog, you do not have to show under him again.

To argue with a judge gets you nowhere!! It is always viewed in poor taste and accomplishes nothing positive. If you have a legitimate complaint, put it in writing and mail it to: Director of Obedience, American Kennel Club, 51 Madison Avenue, New York, New York 10010.

When you lose, congratulate the winner. If for some reason you cannot bring yourself to congratulate the winner, smile and SAY NOTHING!

When you win, *accept* congratulations from others. DO NOT say things like, "Well, he really didn't work that well," or "I know that some of his sits were crooked and the judge didn't see them." This is not good sportsmanship and only degrades the judge who thought enough of your dog to select it as the winner. A simple, "Thank you" is sufficient.

When you feel that you have received a higher score than you deserved, accept it and consider it as a CREDIT. When you feel that you have received a lower score than you deserved, accept it and consider it as a DEBIT. Understand that, in time, the debits and credits balance out and that obedience as a sport really is quite fair.

Appreciate and applaud a good-working dog and/or handler. Then go home and work hard to beat them! If the other guy is a good sport, he will applaud your performance some day.

48

The Bible

IN KEEPING with the analogy that dog training is like a religion, trainers are forever referring to AKC's rule book, their Bible. Like the Bible, the rule book is, on the surface, simply written but open to varied interpretations. I have been involved in obedience for years, and I still refer to the rule book on occasion in the hopes of finding a new explanation for a judge's ruling.

If you are going to play the game, you should know the rules! A copy of the AKC *Obedience Trial Regulations* and a copy of *Guidelines for Obedience Judging* are available free upon request from the AKC by writing to it at 51 Madison Avenue, New York, New York 10010. Unfortunately, after you get done reading both of these booklets, fine points will still elude you. In my classes I "spoon feed" the rules to my students, appraising them of the loopholes and technicalities. What follows is some of the same.

This is not intended to be a recap of the rule book, but there are some things you may not absorb by simply reading the rule book.

While the rule book states that *"judges are not permitted to inject their own variations into the exercises,"* it also gives the judge flexibility by saying, *"The judge must carry a mental picture of the theoretically perfect performance in each exercise and score each dog and handler against this visualized standard . . . ."* It has happened that a dog loses points for no error other than that the dog's performance did not reach the expectations of the judge's mental picture.

No matter how the AKC tries to standardize judging, under the current rules it will always be subject to the judge's opinion. Remember, when you enter a class, you are asking for one person's opinion. If you don't like their opinion, you need not ask for it again.

You are eligible for Novice A only if you have never put a CD title on a dog and have never owned or co-owned a dog that has a CD title, and if you are not a judge. I advise my students to avoid husband-and-wife co-ownerships because if a dog is co-owned and the wife puts a CD on it, her husband will have to show the first dog he actually trains in Novice B.

However, anyone eligible to show in Novice A may, by choice, enter Novice B as in the case where you prefer one judge to another or already have a leg under the Novice A judge.

The AKC says that praise may be given between exercises and following exercises. While this appears clear, there is another rule which says that any form of training in the ring shall be penalized. Be careful *how* you praise your dog and learn which judges are super-sensitive about training in the ring. I was once told that tapping my hip between exercises, to bring the dog to heel position, was "training in the ring." That was one judge's opinion and interpretation of the rules.

On the stand for examination exercise, the rules state that the handler may "*pose the dog as in the show ring.*" A student of mine once received a "0" for this exercise as she lifted her Miniature Schnauzer up off the ground and placed him into a standing position. Of course, the rules also state, "*there shall be a substantial penalty for any dog that is picked up or carried at any time in the obedience ring.*" Does the second statement include posing the dog for a stand? Most judges don't think so; one did. Either way, the score of "0" was incorrect.

While the dog's name may precede any verbal command, an extended pause between the name and command is considered by some judges to be a double command and is penalized.

When calling your dog in Novice, any movement other than your lips (head bob, hands, knees, etc.) is considered an aid to the dog and will be penalized under good judging. In fact, in all of the classes, any extraneous movement that could be considered an aid to the dog is penalized. For example, stopping on about turns to wait for the dog (even if done unconsciously) or giving two drop signals (one as you raise your arm and another as you lower it). The rules clearly state that "*when a signal is permitted and given, it must be a single gesture with one arm and hand only, and the arm must immediately be returned to a natural position.*"

A dog is ineligible to compete if he "*has been changed in appearance by artificial means (except for such changes as are customarily approved for its breed).*" This includes dogs who have had accidents and have needed their tails removed or significantly shortened, as well as corrective eye surgery or hip surgery. Spaying and neutering are not included, and a spayed or neutered animal is allowed to compete in obedience trials.

If you enter a show under a particular judge and later learn that the judge has been changed, you are eligible to receive a cash refund, even if entries have closed, if you plan not to show.

On the long down exercise, the rule book states that handlers shall "*down their dogs to a position facing the opposite side of the ring.*" The rules do not specify *how* the dog is to lie down, only that he is facing the opposite side of the ring. There was once a judge who interpreted this to mean that any dog not in a crouched down should be penalized. He was soon persuaded to change his opinion about this exercise's requirements.

In the retrieve over the high jump exercise, the rules state that "*the handler must stand at least eight feet, or any reasonable distance beyond eight feet, from the jump but must remain in the same spot throughout the exercise, and he must throw the dumbbell at least eight feet beyond the jump.*" Open A handlers have a tendency to want to move their feet *after* they throw the dumbbell. Be careful to *stand still.*

If you throw the dumbbell less than eight feet past the jump or out of the ring or any place else that the judge decides is unacceptable, the judge should return the dumbbell to you and you get a rethrow. While there is nothing in the rules that would indicate a handler should lose points for a rethrow, there are judges who will deduct points, feeling that the handler committed a "handler error" or that the rethrow is in some way an aid to the dog. Here again is a case where interpretation of the written word varies.

Be sure to remove any tags from your dog's collar before showing him.

Judgments and interpretations of the rules seem to run in stages. At one time judges were obsessed with where you held your left hand while heeling, now it is rarely talked about. To keep up with the judging trends, I recommend you subscribe to *FRONT & FINISH, The Dog Trainers News,* P.O. Box 333, Galesburg, Illinois 61402, and to *OFF LEAD Magazine,* P.O. Box 307, Graves Road, Westmoreland, New York 13490. These two periodicals include monthly articles on what is happening in the obedience world.

Know the rules of the game and, just in case, keep your "Bible" with you at all times.

49

Using Match Shows to Your Advantage

ONE OF THE MOST valuable training tools available to a show-oriented person is the match show. All too often match shows are misunderstood or not used to the trainer's advantage.

There are many different kinds of match shows. It is important that the trainer understand each type of match and be familiar with what is and is not permitted.

Match shows fall into two basic categories, sanctioned matches and non-sanctioned matches (also referred to as "fun matches" or "show and go").

The purpose of a sanctioned match is to give the club putting on the match the experience needed for running an obedience trial. The rules for the sanctioned match are not written to benefit the exhibitor. There are two kinds of sanctioned matches, listed as A and B. (An "O" preceding the "A" or "B" refers to "Obedience.") The match regulations that the AKC publishes state that *"There shall be no drilling or intensive or abusive training of dogs on the grounds of an OA or OB sanctioned match."*

The rules for an OB match are a little more lenient than an OA match, which is run just like a trial. *"At Plan OB sanctioned matches, while dogs in the ring may receive verbal corrections, such corrections shall be penalized."* In addition, *"the judge of a Plan OB sanctioned match may, at his own discretion, permit a handler and dog to repeat an exercise; however, only the first performance shall be scored . . . ."*

In general, sanctioned matches are of little value for the obedience trainer. If you are not in a position to correct your dog, you might as well be showing him at a trial! As far as repeating exercises goes, if your dog made a mistake and, for example, went around the high jump on the way back with the dumbbell, why would you want to repeat it? If the dog made the mistake the first time, without a correction or some change made (possibly a simplification), why should he do it right the second time?

Sanctioned matches provide an environment in which handlers get an opportunity to practice their mistakes! I cannot in all honesty recommend to anyone that they show their dog at a match where they are unable to correct. Let the clubs practice giving shows with someone else's dogs! Obedience seminars and workshops would be just as good as fund raisers and would do a lot more to help the training of our dogs.

On the other hand, non-sanctioned matches (fun matches or show-and-go's) are very valuable training experiences. Since these matches are not governed by the AKC, corrections and their restrictions are decided by the group giving the match. I have been to fun matches that permit prong collars, leashes in Open and Utility, food, and all kinds of reasonable corrections in the ring. Under these conditions, the performances of the dogs and handlers can be improved. Problems can be encountered and solved! No prizes are awarded, but the conditions are similar to accredited trials, and the dogs learn to obey in ring situations.

If you live in an area where fun matches are not popular, you can work to change this. It only takes a small group of people to get together on a weekend and set up a ring and play show. Little by little as people realize the value of a fun match, there will be enough people in your area to support a larger match.

Under AKC rules, clubs who are sanctioned to give trials are not permitted to hold non-sanctioned matches. However, the AKC does not restrict these clubs from holding training workshops!!

I do not believe there is such a thing as a "ring-wise dog," that is to say the dog who only makes a mistake when he is in the ring. A dog cannot tell which side of the ring gate he is on, but he can tell if you are nervous or not, and whether he is being compelled to perform.

There is no mistake that cannot be created, you just have to work at it. I had a student whose dog, she said, only laid down on the long sit in a ring. "Really?" I exclaimed questioningly and asked her to sit the dog and leave it. When she had left, I walked over to the dog, pointed to the floor, and commanded "DOWN." The dog dropped immediately. "But that's not fair!" you argue. Sure it is! Is your dog supposed to down because someone in the next ring says "DOWN" and gives a hand signal that your dog sees? It is important that you learn how to cause mistakes because it is only when they occur that you can fix them!

If you walk into a match ring and correct the dog for every little mistake he makes, you have essentially told the dog that this situation is different from a trial. If you have a problem and are using a match to correct the problem, do not correct all the other smaller mistakes the dog might make. Save your correction for the real problem!

Match shows provide an excellent setting in which to train your dog. In fact, some of my best training has been done outside the rings at matches! Training in the midst of show distractions means that when you get results, they will still be there when you cross the gate into the ring.

When training a new dog through titles, match shows help you evaluate your dog's progress and determine when the dog is ready to show. Since match show judges need no special credentials, you are often better off evaluating your own dog or having an instructor evaluate you and your dog than getting a false sense of security from inflated match show scores. Many people who judge matches give out high scores trying to encourage beginners to go on to show. I generally tell my students to subtract five points from their match show score if they want a more realistic idea of their dog's working ability.

When using a match as a training experience, ask to show FEO (for exhibition only). If the judge understands that you are only for exhibition and are in no way competing, he is more likely to allow you to correct since he doesn't have to worry about how to score you. Showing FEO should also allow you to enter one dog in many levels, e.g. Novice, Open and Utility.

While every beginner looks forward to their first ribbon, let it be a blue one from a trial and not a pink one from a match! (Yes, match ribbons are issued in different colors, so you are never going to fool anybody!) Take advantage of your fun matches to have fun improving your dog's performances. Practice makes perfect, *as long as you practice the right way!*

50

The Week Before the Show

THE WEEK BEFORE you show your dog, take special care to make sure your dog's ears are free from dirt or infection, his anal glands are not full, his hair is not in his eyes and he is free of external and internal parasites. Any one of these things could cause problems in the ring.

With assured health, now turn your attention toward your dog's attitude. For very "high," energetic dogs, make sure the dog gets plenty of exercise the week and day of the show. Sometimes with the hyper dogs, we kid about taking them to the show tied to the bumper of the car! Some dogs need to have lots of exercise before they can settle down enough to perform in a ring. I know of one exhibitor who gets to a show four hours early to give his dog time to unwind!

On the other hand, if your dog has limited energy, you will want to keep the dog confined to a crate and resting a good part of the week before the show. For some dogs, no training at all the day before a show is the best way to go. If your dog tires easily, get him to sleep early the night before— no late night TV!

It is my policy to never change anything the week before a show. If you're not happy with your dog's response to a verbal down command, now is not the time to switch to a hand signal.

Be careful not to over-train or over-correct your dog just because you have a show coming up. If anything, train in shorter, happy sessions, working on problem areas and on polishing (i.e. fronts and finishes). Have you heard people say, "He was doing great until I mailed the entry in"? It is not uncommon to see handlers become tense and panicky because they mailed in an entry, and this is bound to affect the dog. Remember, no one forces you to go to a show, even if you are entered. Since we have to enter weeks in advance, sometimes we miscalculate our dog's readiness, and the week before the show we find he is not. If you don't feel confident about taking your dog into the ring, then lose the entry money and stay home. Relax and go back to training. You are never penalized for not showing. Consider it a donation to a worthy cause. Many have made such donations.

Some dogs need food in their stomachs or they get ill. Others work better on a totally empty stomach. As a quick "pick-up" or energy boost, try giving your lethargic dog honey water 15 minutes before you show. Experiment with feeding and its effect on your dog's performance at matches before you get to the trials. For fear of bloat, a dog should not eat a full meal and then jump sooner than four hours later.

Experiment with playing with your dog versus drilling your dog before you go into the ring. Each dog will require a different kind of warm-up to get ready for the ring. Match shows offer you a chance to try different kinds of warm-ups to see what works best to put your dog in a good thinking, attentive, alert frame of mind for the ring.

51

As You Train
Your First Advanced Dog

IF YOU CONTINUE on with training past beginners, certain situations are bound to occur:

- You will have good training sessions with your dog where you finish feeling satisfied and happy.
- You will have lousy training sessions with your dog where you finish feeling frustrated and irritated. (Try not to let the dog know it.)
- You will make numerous mistakes in your training.
- You will be corrected by your instructors—some days more than others.
- From time to time you will feel that "you know better" and you will not adhere to the recommendations of your instructors.
- You will find yourself unfairly comparing your dog to others in the class.
- Occasionally you will become angry with your instructors and your classmates.
- There will be days when you feel like giving up, but for some reason you don't. That's because down deep you know you and your dog can do it.
- There will be exercises you don't practice as much as others because *you* don't enjoy doing them.
- There will be days when you wonder if your life really has room for dog training.

I know. I have been a student much longer than I have been an instructor. I am still a student. Anyone who trains has felt all of these things at one time or another. Some encouraging words:

- All you have to do is want a degree badly enough and you will achieve it. Your determination is a lot stronger than even the most difficult dog.

- No mistake you ever make while training your dog is irreversible. Dogs *re*train very well.
- Your second and third dogs will be better than your first. Each dog will teach you to be a better trainer.
- With every conflict you face in training—whether it is with your dog, your instructor, your classmates or your spouse—you are learning. Of course, you may not realize it at the time.

Dog training is a unique and wonderful sport. It spans all ages, all life styles, all economies and includes both sexes. It stimulates the mind as well as the body. It teaches compassion as well as sportsmanship. Dog training strengthens patience and understanding of yourself, your dog and others around you. Once you leave beginners, dog training takes on a new perspective. View the problems and stumbling blocks as growth. Accept the conflicts as learning experiences.

"Nothing worth doing is easy." So train on . . . .

52

"As Told by the Dog" or
"It's a Dog's Life?"

SHE TOLD ME to "SIT" and "STAY," and I did. She walked away from me as she had done many times before. She had a long leash in her hand. I sat comfortably, proud of myself for understanding. All of a sudden it happened! My neck hurt and I was propelled across the room. Sometime while flying through the air I heard her say, "COME." When I arrived at her feet, she told me I was a "Good puppy"; mistreated would have been more appropriate! Still attached to the long leash, I had a horrible thought: she was taking me back to do it again.

* * * * *

I was lying relaxed at his feet; the instructor was talking, but I didn't understand the big words. All of a sudden it happened. He snapped me off the floor and took off towards the center of the room. Ouch! That hurt! Why didn't he just tell me to Heel? I would have been more than happy to. I guess his sudden move meant that we were next in the class to perform the exercise. Was I supposed to know that?

* * * * *

We were working dumbbell. She threw the dumbbell and sent me. The command "TAKE IT" rang loud and clear. I trotted right out and found that there were two dumbbells, mine and another one. The other one was bigger, newer, and was painted white on the ends. I picked up the bright, new, shiny dumbbell and brought it back to her. She was not happy.

She threw my dumbbell again. I waited anxiously for the command. "TAKE IT," she exclaimed, and I headed straight out. Just then she started to say something to me. I turned to go back to find out what she wanted, and all of a sudden she pinched my ear! Next time I guess I just won't listen to what she says; it gets me into trouble.

* * * * *

He threw the dumbbell. I trotted out to get it, my tail waving high. I picked it up and spotted the high jump. Wanting to please, I jumped the high jump on my way back to him. All of a sudden there was a blood-curdling scream, "NO!" That's funny, I thought; the last time I jumped the jump, he had really been pleased with me.

* * * * *

Her hand went up and I dropped to the ground. "Good," she commented. Then her other hand made some funny motion that I have never seen before. I stayed down, not knowing what else to do. She walked back to me with an angry scowl and snapped me up, insisting "SIT." Was I supposed to know that?

* * * * *

He commanded "COME," and I briskly trotted toward him. When I got there, I sat, and he kicked me! "Straight," he kept repeating. Finally he gave up, and he set me up to do it again. He called me and I came, but not too close for I didn't know if his foot might be ready to kick. "NO," he exclaimed. I guess he really didn't want me to come. He set me up a third time. This time he called me and I stayed put. He came at me with an angry look, and I was frightened. I headed in the other direction, and he got even louder. "Come over here," were the words he used, but I had never heard that as a command before, so I kept going. I think he will get over it. He gets like this every now and then. Maybe he just had a bad day?

* * * * *

Do we give enough thought to how our dogs perceive our corrections? I think not.

53

What May Have Caused This Problem?

RESEARCH INDICATES that no action by a dog is uncaused. When we relate this to training, it means that if your dog consistently gives you undesired behavior, it is likely a reaction to something you are doing. Sometimes, more important than correcting the behavior is to eliminate the cause of it.

Below is a list of common obedience problems that are more often than not "handler caused."

1. **Every time you halt, the dog leans on your left leg. What may have caused the problem?**

   Dogs develop the habit of leaning on a handler's leg when the handler praises the dog by petting the dog's head into his leg. To avoid this leaning problem, pet the dog on the chest for a good straight sit at heel. Lack of confidence on the part of the dog might also cause him to hug your leg for security.

2. **When the dog is excited, he continues to circle the handler before calming down enough to sit at heel. What may have caused this circling behavior?**

   Handlers sometimes get into a habit of heeling the dog in a circle (usually to the right if the handler is right-handed) to position the dog for an exercise. The circling problem can be avoided if the handler will vary circling to the right with circling to the left and eventually teach the dog to back up, move sideways, and make other minor adjustments into position.

3. **In beginners class, the dog is forging. By Novice, he is lagging. What may have caused the problem?**

   Lagging is often the result of giving praise at the wrong time and improper lead corrections. Too often handlers, in an attempt to encourage their dogs up into Heel position, in effect praise them for lagging. Many problems are created when the handler snaps instead of tight-leading in an attempt to get the dog to move up into Heel position. Snapping up clips the dog with the snap of the leash under the chin, and he tends to lag even farther behind. The best rule is not to give a dog enough leash to lag in early training.

4. A dog frequently sits at heel with his head next to his handler's left leg and his rear out away from the handler. What may have caused this crooked sit?

This is usually caused by petting the dog into your leg or by snapping the lead across your body instead of straight up over the dog's head to get him to sit. The snap across your body pulls the dog's head into your side, forcing his hind end out away from you.

5. A dog sits just out of reach after doing a recall. What may have caused this?

This is usually a result of the handler who reached out for his dog when first teaching the recall. Always let the dog *touch you first!* Keep your hands to yourself!

6. A dog consistently forges on sits. What may have caused it?

This is usually caused when a handler stops positioning the dog into perfect Heel position in early training too soon. The dog does not really understand where Heel position is and is not catching the cue to stop. Some handlers stop too abruptly, making it impossible for the dog to anticipate a halt. A dog who is not paying attention will miss the cue to stop. In this case, don't worry about the sit; fix the attention.

7. A dog runs past his handler on recall. What may have caused this?

The dog never made the decision to stop at the handler when the recall was first taught on leash. The handler probably restrained the dog with the leash and did not allow him to run past and find out what happens. Go back on leash and allow the dog to run past. When he does, snap him again back toward you. Make sure the leash is loose after the snap. It must be the dog's decision to stop by you; to restrain him only teaches him that he is on leash.

8. A dog does not change pace with the handler. What may have caused this?

The dog probably does not understand the change of pace. This happens when the handler does not exaggerate the slow and the fast enough in training. Often the handler does not maintain the different paces for a long enough period of time. To teach the slow, go very slowly for a considerable distance. To teach the fast, jog with your dog! Maintain a steady rhythm at all paces.

9. A dog does not respond on the first command to "DOWN." What may have caused this?

The handler probably commanded the dog more than once instead of enforcing the first command. Now the dog waits to see which command will be enforced.

10. A dog sits when the handler returns on the stand for examination. What may have caused this?

This can be caused by sitting the dog directly after a stand. The dog anticipates the end of the exercise and sits. It is better to heel the dog out of a stand after you praise for the stand. If the sit is submissive, it is usually because the handler has over-corrected the dog on the stand. If the handler attempted to correct the stand with the use of the leash, he may have snapped up, and the dog's interpretation of the upward motion by the leash is to sit.

11. A dog is nervous and spooky on long sits and downs. What may have caused this?

Some dogs, because of their breed or lines within the breed, are born with a tendency to be nervous and spooky. These dogs need lots of socialization when they are young to build their confidence in the world. More often than not, shaky sits and downs are a result of training where the handlers gained distance too quickly when first teaching the exercises. A better approach would have been to stay in close and proof the dog for steadiness around distractions. The handler who overlooks minor movement in stays is asking for trouble later on!

54

Preparing for a Tournament

OBEDIENCE TOURNAMENTS like the Gaines Regionals and Classics and the World Series are competitions where the dog and handler team is judged multiple times and their final score is based on an average of the individual performances. In the Superdog division of the Gaines events, each team shows in Open three times and in Utility three times over a two-day period. Preparing a dog for this strenuous type of competition is very different from getting ready for a weekend of showing, where each class produces a separate score.

In tournament competition, a single major error usually puts you out of the placements. Because of this, consistency becomes more important than the perfection of any individual exercise. I have witnessed many good dogs, capable of very high scores on any given weekend, fall apart at competitions because the handlers pressure the dogs for perfection to the point where the dogs tire and lose concentration. While it may be true that at an individual show in a competitive Open B class the winner is likely to be decided on one front or finish, such is not usually the case in tournament competitions.

Keeping a dog alert, attentive and "up" over two days of showing in six classes requires special training. Preparation for a major tournament begins about three months before the event.

I do not believe that it is possible for a dog or person to perform to their uppermost limits all of the time. Believing that you can always do your best is overly idealistic and unrealistic. Knowing this, I try to gear the dog towards a competition, working so that if I am careful, the dog will *peak* the weekend of the important show.

For the first month of tournament training, all pressure for perfection is removed from the dog. All efforts go into training for stamina. I want the dog so mentally and physically prepared that he or she will sail through six classes easily with energy to spare. Stamina training includes extensive exercise, only some of which is related to obedience. I swim my dogs, run them and jump them on grass repeatedly. By setting the jumps in a circle, the dog can be taught to jump in and out in a circle continuously. Gradually the number of jumps the dog executes in a row is increased. In-and-out jumping increases timing and builds muscles. (Be sure to jump the dog in both directions.)

Training sessions at this time become long. Each time the dog is worked just a little beyond the point where he starts to show signs of being tired. When stamina is really strong and weather conditions are good, it is not unreasonable to work a dog 1½ to two hours at a time. Mentally the dog can handle this workout since there is very little stress. The dog is not learning anything new and there is no pressure for accuracy.

An example of a stamina program would be to work on just exercise (jumping, swimming or running) one day, the next day work obedience exercises, and the third day rest the dog. This sequence is then repeated.

Stamina practice continues at matches where the dog is entered (for exhibition only) numerous times. The goal is to be able to qualify in six classes in one day at a match. When this is accomplished, mastering six classes over a two-day tournament will seem easy to both the dog and handler. Match practice gives the dog the experience of running from one ring directly into another ring to perform the stay exercises. This is also a training period where the handler learns how much his dog is capable of giving and how to pace him through multiple classes.

During the second month of preparation, stamina training is slowly decreased and proof training is introduced. Now the dog is stressed to think but at the same time he is no longer being worked for long periods of time at once. Any weak links or possible areas of confusion should be sorted out at this time. If at all possible, we try to avoid the stress of proofing just before the important show. Depending on the dog and his experience, proofing may continue up to two weeks before the tournament. The more weak links in training, the longer you would continue proof training, except if the dog is extremely stressed by proofing.

At the beginning of the third month, accuracy is gently added. It is here where fronts, finishes and sits are redone. Doodling becomes a big part of a training session.

Depending on the dog, the accuracy training may continue as late as two weeks before the big event. It is during the last two weeks of training that we work specifically on building the dog's ego and confidence. Exercises are relatively simple. Praise is profuse. Training sessions are very brief (10-20 minutes). The next to the last week before the show the dog is rested more days than he is trained. Rest and brief positive sessions continue up to the day of the show. In the last week of training, accuracy is dealt with less and less as consistency and attitude become more important.

It can be very disappointing to have a dog injure himself just before a long-awaited event. In preparation for the big event, the handler should be more cautious than ever to avoid injuries. Playing with groups of other dogs should be avoided. Postpone swimming in strange waters where glass or cans might cut pads. In general, be very careful to keep the dog healthy before a tournament. A little caution is worthwhile.

Traveling to a show can be stressful. Be sure to allow enough time at the other end of the trip for the dog to adjust and acclimate to new temperatures and altitudes. Four days is an ideal time for this to occur.

Many people are afraid to fly their dogs. Personally I have flown many dogs many times and have had no major problems. Of course, it takes a little care and common sense to master flying. I would never fly a dog who had to switch planes. By always arranging a direct, non-stop flight, I avoid the risk that the dog will be shipped to the wrong place. When boarding, I always wait to see the dog boarded before I go aboard. If it is impossible to see this occur, I ask the flight attendant at the desk in front of the boarding area to radio to the freight people and see if a dog of whatever breed has been loaded. I mark my crate with arrows and special designs so that it is easy to describe as well as locate from a distance.

When landing, I again wait until I *see* the dog taken off of the plane before I deplane. If there is a problem, stewardesses are contacted. Since they are usually anxious for me to get off the plane, they are very helpful in locating the dog.

The dog's crate is lined with a thick quilt to absorb vibration and afford the dog traction. It is soft so that should the crate be turned upside down there is nothing hard to hit him in the head.

The biggest problem dogs face when flying is the noise of the runways and engines. For the past five years I have found it very successful to plug the dog's ears with cotton before putting him in the crate. Of course, once you land, remember to remove the cotton!

The dog flies with a loosely fitted buckle collar with I.D. attached! If the collar should get caught on some part of the crate, the dog could easily slip out of it.

I have always felt that an hour and a half plane ride is, in the long run, less stressful and exhausting for me and the dog than a 10 or more hour car ride. Flying can be safe and fun if you exercise some care and preparation.

As the big day draws near, it is crucial that the handler not allow his nerves to upset the dog. Mistakes made the month before the show are often handled correctly. Unfortunately, when mistakes occur a day or two before the big tournament (and they will!), handlers often over-react and unnecessarily upset the dog.

It is important to remember that when it comes to tournaments, it is often the steady, good working dog that places over the erratic but extremely flashy and often precise dog.

Any individual class at a dog show may be won or lost with a single crooked sit. Such is not the case in tournament competitions. When a single crooked sit is averaged over six shows, it really doesn't affect the final outcome. Good tournament trainers know this and ignore minor errors. They concentrate on building an attentive, alert, confident, winning attitude in the dog.

55

The Relationship

FOR CENTURIES man and dog have experienced a special relationship. Dog has worked for man and with man continuously. Whether it is sheep herding, hunting, protection, guiding the blind, assisting the impaired or merely performing circus tricks or obedience, the capabilities of dog as man's friend and employee appear endless.

Knowing how devoted, trusting and hard-working a dog can be, it seems tragically simplistic for people to think that the only way to get a dog to perform simple obedience tasks is to either bribe him with food or repeatedly force him with corrections. What has happened to the relationship with "man's best friend" in obedience training? Do dogs today no longer wish to please?

I believe the problem stems from the trainers who do not take the time to build a relationship with their dogs before and throughout training. It takes less time and very little thought to correct a dog whenever it does not perform. Understanding a dog, reading a dog and *teaching* a dog in a step-by-step process take time and thought. Trainers need to be encouraged to give more time to *thinking* about how they train.

A sound working relationship is built on trust, honesty and mutual respect. The dog over time learns to totally trust his trainer. He knows that the trainer will not put him in an unsafe situation nor ask him to do something dangerous. For example, the dog trusts that if told to stay, it is safe to do so. If told to jump (e.g. over a strange jump in a new location), the dog trusts he will not encounter any "dragons" living on the other side. The dog trusts that if sent to retrieve, there is in fact something to be retrieved. The dog must know that the trainer will not arbitrarily correct him, nor correct him for what he has not yet learned. When a confused dog is corrected, he learns to fear instead of trust.

If you hand your dog over to someone else to work, or even worse to correct, you destroy trust. Suppose your spouse or sibling handed you over to a stranger and said, "She won't listen to me. Here, see what you can do with her!"

Chapter 4 explains the importance of honesty in a training relationship. Telling a dog that he is correct when he is wrong confuses him. Correcting a dog automatically, before he has made a mistake, is dishonest and unfair. Threatening to correct, as in squeezing his ear just before you send him to retrieve, is equally unfair.

There are many dishonest training methods in use today. It is my belief that while such dishonest methods may temporarily solve a training problem, they often cause more serious problems later on since they destroy the training relationship.

Trainers talk a lot about how important it is for a dog to respect his master. This is true. It is equally important for the trainer to respect his dog!

Not long ago it came to my attention that I cannot earn an obedience title without the dog, and he cannot earn one without me. This makes us equally important. Viewing the dog as an equal partner sheds new light on the training picture. It suggests that the dog has rights.

While it may be my right to issue a command to the dog, it is the dog's right to say he doesn't understand, and it then becomes my obligation to listen to my partner. As a partner with rights, what the dog says is just as important to our relationship as what I say. Since dogs do not speak English, however, it is easy to tune them out. This would be very detrimental to the training relationship. If a friend of yours never listened to what you had to say, would you choose to continue to work with this person? Dogs talk with body language. The good trainer learns to read and speak "dog" fluently.

There are certain things that I don't do to my dog, and certain things my dog does not do to me. This understanding works as follows: For example, I do not command my dog to perform a sit-stay exercise in the bright sun when the temperature is over 90 degrees. In return, when I do command my dog to do a sit-stay, she does it.

It is your responsibility as a partner to protect your dog from unbearable and unsafe show conditions. If an obedience ring does not have adequate matting for safe jumping, you are better off pulling your entry than running the risk of injuring the dog and breaking the bond of trust you have worked so hard to build.

When you respect your dog, you believe in him. You give him credit for having the intelligence to perform obedience and exercises and you allow him the right to make the mistakes necessary for learning. The dog allows you to make mistakes in teaching, so why not afford him the same consideration.

Building the relationship I speak of requires putting your feelings of superiority and your ego on a shelf and working *with* the dog as a partner. If you are busy proving to the dog that you know how to do the exercise correctly and he doesn't, you are "barking up the wrong tree." Satisfying your need to feel superior by repeatedly telling the dog he is wrong does not encourage him to want to work with you. The essence of obedience is not who can force whom to do what, but rather how can we work together to learn obedience so that in the end we will develop into a smooth, stylish, happy team in the ring.

This book is a combination of philosophy and technique. I suggest to you that the most expert training techniques available are of little value if there is no spirit of cooperation to begin with.

To build a special relationship with your dog, start with honesty, trust and respect. To this add patience, thought, and room for error. Do not hesitate to be demanding, but do so fairly and with kindness. When you have completed this recipe for love, add a touch of technique, and mail in your entry!

APPENDIX

FOR A FREE COPY of the booklet *Obedience Regulations,* write to: The American Kennel Club, Inc., 51 Madison Avenue, New York, New York 10010.

Levels of AKC obedience competition, the exercises at each level, and the titles earned are as follows:

NOVICE CLASS

Novice Exercises and Scores: The exercises and maximum scores in the Novice classes are:

1. Heel on Leash and Figure Eight ....40 points
2. Stand for Examination ....30 points
3. Heel Free ....40 points
4. Recall ....30 points
5. Long Sit ....30 points
6. Long Down ....30 points
   Maximum Total Score ....200 points

C.D. Title: The American Kennel Club will issue a Companion Dog certificate for each registered dog, and will permit the use of the letters "C.D." after the name of each dog that has been certified by three different judges to have received qualifying scores in Novice classes at three licensed or member obedience trials, provided the sum total of dogs that actually competed in the regular Novice classes at each trial is not less than six.

OPEN CLASS

Open Exercises and Scores: The exercises and maximum scores in the n classes are:

1. Heel Free and Figure Eight ....40 points
2. Drop on Recall ....30 points
3. Retrieve on Flat................................20 points
4. Retrieve over High Jump ....30 points
5. Broad Jump ....20 points
   Long Sit ....30 points
   Long Down ....30 points
   Maximum Total Score ....200 points

C.D.X. Title: The American Kennel Club will issue a Companion Dog Excellent certificate for each registered dog, and will permit the use of the letters "C.D.X." after the name of each dog that has been certified by three different judges of obedience trials to have received qualifying scores in Open classes at three licensed or member obedience trials, provided the sum total of dogs that actually competed in the regular Open classes at each trial is not less than six.

UTILITY CLASS

Utility Exercises and Scores: The exercises, maximum scores and order of judging in the Utility classes are:

1. Signal Exercise....................................40 points
2. Scent Discrimination, Article No. 1 ....30 points
3. Scent Discrimination, Article No. 2 ....30 points
4. Directed Retrieve.................................30 points
5. Directed Jumping ....40 points
6. Group Examination ....30 points
   Maximum Total Score ....200 points

U.D. Title: The American Kennel Club will issue a Utility Dog certificate for each registered dog, and will permit the use of the letters "U.D." after the name of each dog that has been certified by three different judges of obedience trials to have received qualifying scores in Utility classes at three licensed or member obedience trials in each of which three or more dogs actually competed in the Utility class or classes.

O.T. Ch. Title: The Obedience Trial Champion title is earned after earning the U.D. title. Championship points are accumulated from placements in the Open and Utility classes.

c

Ope

6.
7.
M.